MYTHS

— and —

LEGENDS

of the World

MYTHS

and

LEGENDS

of the World

retold by **ALLI BRYDON**   illustrated by **JULIA IREDALE**

CONTENTS

WELCOME TO THE WORLD OF

MYTHS
— and —
LEGENDS

Bold reader: open your mystical map and get ready to travel through time with 21 dazzling stories of adventure, deceit, reward, and punishment. These myths and legends will transport you to regions from every corner of the globe: Africa, Europe, Asia, Oceania, the Americas, and the Arctic. Journey from ancient to modern times, from hot climates to freezing temperatures, from mountaintops to seafloors. Meet gods, goddesses, and demigods; move alongside serpents, coyotes, talking fish, and clever spiders; cavort with sea nymphs, mystical women, terrifying beasts, and volcano-people. Hear different versions of how the world began.

The book you now hold in your hands links you to many generations; some of these tales have even been passed down through a long line of oral traditions. Do not step lightly into this reading adventure! The souls of ancestors, the lives of heroes, and the fates of mortals are in your grasp. Be alert, bold traveler, and read on!

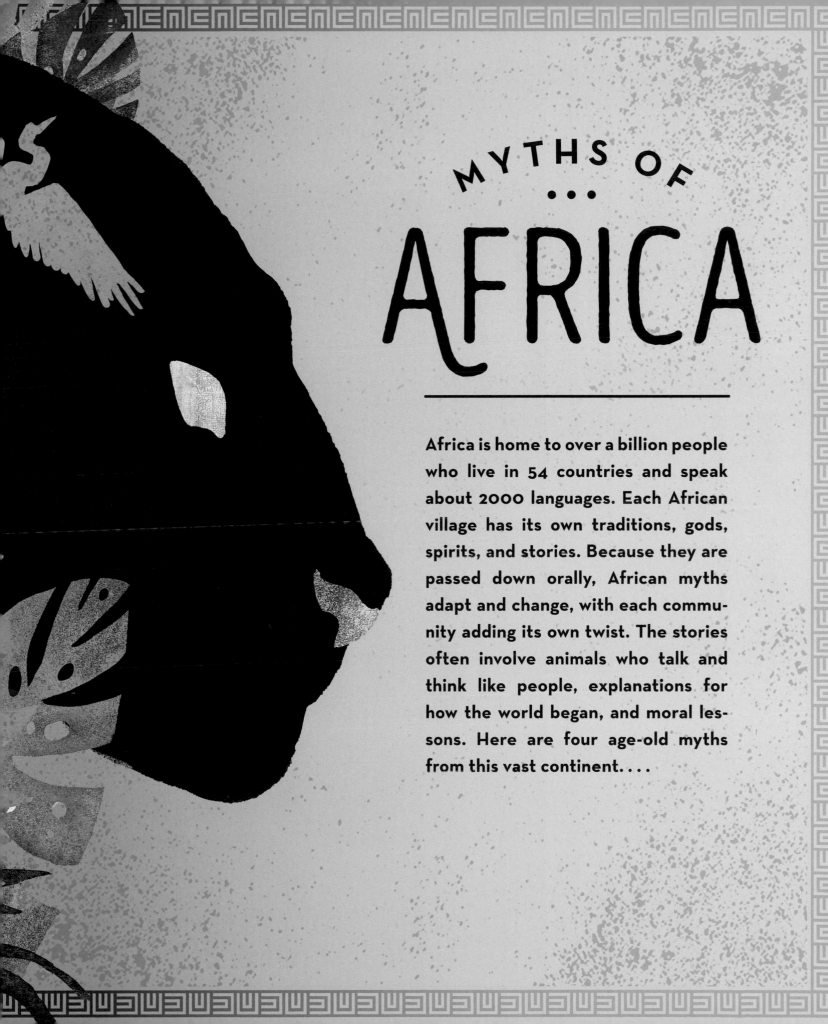

MYTHS OF

...

AFRICA

Africa is home to over a billion people who live in 54 countries and speak about 2000 languages. Each African village has its own traditions, gods, spirits, and stories. Because they are passed down orally, African myths adapt and change, with each community adding its own twist. The stories often involve animals who talk and think like people, explanations for how the world began, and moral lessons. Here are four age-old myths from this vast continent. . . .

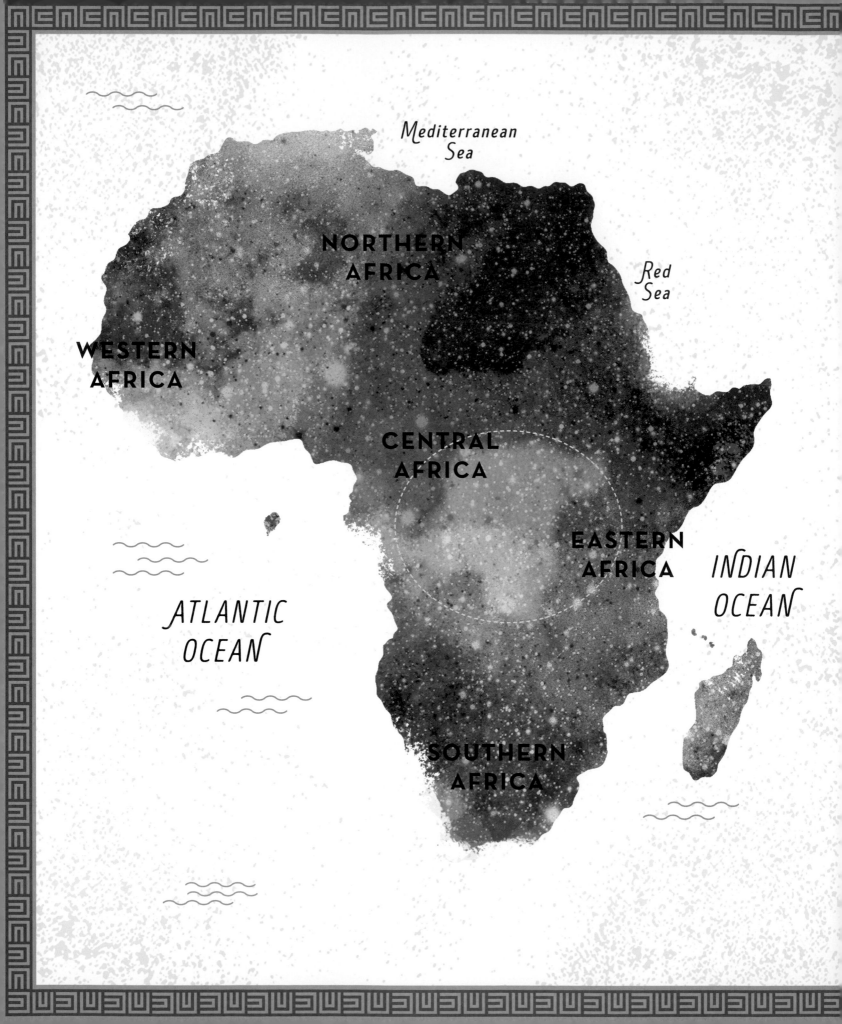

The Creation of the World

FROM THE KUBA PEOPLE OF PRESENT-DAY
DEMOCRATIC REPUBLIC OF CONGO

The great and powerful Mbombo sat alone in the middle of the vast, dark Earth. Ancient black waters rushed around his human-like form. Mbombo felt very ill. In fact, he had been feeling ill for millions of years, due to loneliness. He felt this sad solitude in the pit of his stomach, and the sickening feeling had intensified over eons until it became painful. Mbombo's belly had also grown bigger and bigger, until finally he vomited.

From deep within Mbombo's belly came the sun, which rose into the sky and scattered light everywhere. Next he vomited the moon, stars, and all the other planets. Then the bright, hot sun evaporated some of the ancient water on Earth, creating clouds which then, in turn, rained back down on the land. In time, hills emerged from the water like enormous, dry waves.

But Mbombo was not finished; he still felt very ill. It was a wrenching, rolling, terrible pain. Just as Mbombo thought he'd get no relief, he vomited once more, bringing nine animals into existence: THE LEOPARD, called Koy Bumba; THE EAGLE, Ponga Bumba; THE CROCODILE, Ganda Bumba; THE FISH, Yo Bumba; THE TORTOISE, Kono Bumba; THE SWIFT, BLACK LEOPARD-LIKE CREATURE MADE OF LIGHTNING, Tsetse Bumba; THE WHITE HERON, Nyanyi Bumba; THE SCARAB BEETLE with no name; and THE GOAT named Budi.

And yet, Mbombo still felt he had to vomit more. Flowing out of his wide mouth came many men and many women to keep him company on Earth. Now, that's what he had needed! Mbombo felt a lot better, and his stomach was calm and pleasant again.

Now Mbombo was able to sit back and relax, as his creations began forming all the rest of the world's creatures. The jewel-colored scarab beetle went on to make all the other insects in the world, countless numbers of them. The graceful white heron, Nyanyi Bumba, bowed its long beak and created all the birds to grace the sky—all but one: the kite. The toothy crocodile, Ganda Bumba, called into being all the scaly creatures, like snakes and lizards, to slither across the Earth. Yo Bumba, the fish, populated the seas with tens of thousands of other fish. Lastly, Budi, the sturdy-footed goat, created all the horned animals to roam the land.

Three of Mbombo's sons came forward to help their father finish creating the world. The first son, Nyonye Ngana, vomited out white ants but died soon after. His little alabaster-colored ants mourned and sought to bury him in the dark dirt underground. Working together, they tunneled down, eventually turning dry sand into rich soil. Thus, the people were able to farm.

Coincidentally, around the same time his brother perished, another of Mbombo's sons, Chonganda, created all the plants: tall trees, verdant bushes, dense grasses, multicolored flowers, and crops of all kinds. So, the people took this opportunity to reap the benefits of bountiful farms. And a third son, Chedi Bumba, created the last bird, the fierce kite, a bird of prey.

Man, woman, and animal now lived together in harmony, with kindness and respect for each other—all but the swift, black leopard-like creature made of lightning, Tsetse Bumba. Tsetse Bumba ran through villages and forests, setting them on fire. He was nothing but trouble! Mbombo banished Tsetse Bumba to the sky and turned him into a lightning bolt: swift and hot and dangerous. But, thankfully, now far away and infrequent. From time to time, Tsetse Bumba still causes trouble and disobeys Mbombo, flashing down to Earth and setting fire to villages and forests.

Now that Earth was mostly peaceful, and Mbombo saw that his work was finished, he retreated into the heavens to rest. He bestowed the responsibility of Earth upon another of his sons, Loko Yima, and happily left him in charge.

MBOMBO HAS NEVER HAD ANOTHER STOMACHACHE SINCE.

THE TALE OF THE
Ghosts
and the
Flutes

FROM THE BEBA PEOPLE OF CAMEROON

In the middle of a forest, there was a small village where two widows, Manda and Ngonda, lived with their young sons. Manda had her son Kweni, and Ngonda had her son Chebe. The women and their boys were as different from each other as sun and moon, north and south, desert and sea.

You see, Manda and Kweni were humble and hardworking. They toiled daily and without complaint in the sun-scorched fields. They respected everything around them—their fellow villagers, all of Earth's creatures, and the blessed land on which they lived. But Ngonda and her son, Chebe, were of a different kind: they were lazy and greedy. Those two put in as little effort as possible and stole moments of rest when it was time to work. They took more than their share of food and water when it was time for everyone to eat and drink.

Every morning, as the pink sky welcomed the early sun, all the women and children in the village walked together to a distant farm to work. The women got their hands dirty, planting and harvesting the crops, while the boys and girls played bamboo flutes to entertain and sustain them. Melodies from the children mixed with the women's grunts and breaths. The sun arced above the workers and shone down upon their wrapped heads.

To escape the heat of the midday sun, the women and children rested in the old farmhouse. As they cooled off and drank water, Kweni asked his mother, "Why do we race home every day, even before the sun dips low in the sky? Isn't there more work to be done?"

"Loyal child, we cannot be here after dark. This farm is ruled by ghosts at nightfall," Manda told her son.

Chebe pondered Manda's reply. As he reached for another cool drink, the lazy child asked his mother, "Mama, if there are ghosts here at night, why don't we leave now? It's getting late enough. Surely today's work can be done tomorrow!"

Mediterranean Sea

NORTHERN AFRICA

WESTERN AFRICA

Red Sea

CENTRAL AFRICA

EASTERN AFRICA

ATLANTIC OCEAN

SOUTHERN AFRICA

"My child, we must all walk back together for safety, otherwise you and I would certainly leave early," Ngonda said as she shuddered at the thought of ghosts.

That afternoon, when the group had almost reached their village, Kweni realized he had left his bamboo flute in the old farmhouse.

"I must go back and get it!" he said, for it was a very special flute.

Kweni's father had hand-carved it for him shortly before he died. The music it made filled the empty space in his heart. He cherished it more than anything.

"No, my son. You mustn't go back. The ghosts will be coming out soon," Manda implored him. "You can get it tomorrow."

But Kweni could not bear the thought of being without his precious flute, and he was worried the ghosts might steal it if he left it there all night long. So he turned and ran back to the farmhouse, trying to overcome the fear in his heart.

When he arrived at the farm, the night was dark and the moon was a scant crescent. Kweni could barely see his hand in front of his face, but when he entered the farmhouse, he saw many ghosts. They were glowing in the darkness and sitting in a circle.

"Child!" the Chief Ghost shrieked at Kweni, and it made him jump. "Why do you bother us at night?"

"I left my flute here," Kweni said. He could barely speak the words, he was trembling so much. "I—need—it—back," he chattered through his teeth.

The ghosts looked at each other and grinned with sly crescent moons.

"We have many flutes here," the Chief Ghost said. "Beautiful ones. Precious ones. Come over here and tell me which one is yours."

Following the Chief Ghost into the next room, Kweni suddenly stopped, dazzled. He saw dozens of flutes floating before his eyes. Flutes of silver, flutes of gold, and flutes studded with diamonds and rubies. They glittered almost as brightly as the ghosts.

"This one is mine," he said, plucking the bamboo flute from the air and placing it gently into his raffia bag.

The Chief Ghost's crescent grin turned upside down.

"Well, child," said the ghost, "so there it is! For your troubles, let us give you a gift before you go home. Come with me and choose a special pot to take with you."

In the next room, Kweni saw pots of all shapes and sizes. There were pots of gold, pots of silver, and pots studded with diamonds and rubies. Which one should he pick? His mother had taught him never to be greedy.

"I will take this pot," he said, and he picked up the smallest one. It was about the size of his head and made of plain metal. The ghosts surely wouldn't miss this pot if he took it. Then he ran back home, almost as quickly as he came.

His mother was overjoyed to see him arrive home safely.

"My child is home from the ghosts!" Manda cried and wrapped Kweni in her arms.

Kweni told his mother all about his visit with the ghosts. He showed her his precious flute and gave her the metal pot.

"What is this for, Kweni?"

The boy shrugged and told her the ghosts had wanted to give him a parting gift. "And I want to give it to you," he told his mother.

Curious and wary, Manda slowly

removed the lid. To their surprise, all kinds of wondrous things jumped out! Bags of spices, sweet pumpkins, beautiful black robes embroidered with colorful wool, sharp steel axes, carved mahogany walking sticks, finely crafted sandals, and cowrie shell necklaces. Even baby goats and piglets jumped out of the pot! There were so many things to enjoy and use—it was an embarrassment of riches. So Manda gave away much of the bounty to her fellow villagers and to any visitors who came to their humble home. It seemed everyone in the village was happy for the new riches . . .

. . . EXCEPT FOR NGONDA.

She was jealous of Manda's pot. And she had an idea.

"Tomorrow, leave your flute at the farmhouse," she told Chebe. "After nightfall, go back to retrieve it. But instead of taking your bamboo flute, pick a gold one instead. And bring me back the biggest pot they have, one with diamonds and rubies. If so many good things came out of Manda's tiny, modest pot, imagine the riches that will come out of a big, lavish one!"

Chebe reluctantly did as he was told. He wasn't really up for the task, being quite a lazy boy, but he did want all those riches for his mother and himself. So he left his bamboo flute at the farmhouse the next day, then returned to get it at night.

When the Chief Ghost asked him which flute was his, the boy said it was the golden one as he grabbed it. When the ghost offered him a choice of pots to take home, Chebe chose one so large and laden with jewels that he could hardly carry it back home.

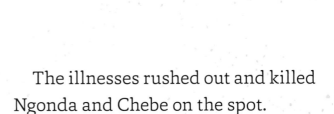

Ngonda was delighted as she saw her son struggling home with the most opulent pot she had ever seen. Her skin tingled at the thought of the riches that would soon be hers. Chebe stumbled in with the pot and Ngonda shut the door firmly behind them. She didn't want any of the villagers to see what came out of the pot—she wanted to keep it all for herself and Chebe.

Greedily, she lifted the lid of the enormous pot. But instead of delightful surprises, Ngonda and Chebe received horrors! All the illnesses of the world came flying out of the large, jeweled pot.

· ·

MALARIA.

YELLOW FEVER.

LEPROSY.

CHICKEN POX.

MEASLES.

· ·

The illnesses rushed out and killed Ngonda and Chebe on the spot.

Later the same day, an old man from the village knocked on Ngonda and Chebe's door. The man was worried about them; their home had been shut all day, and that was unusual in their lively village. As he forced open the door to check on them, little bits of the illnesses flew outside through the small crack right over his head. The man quickly realized what was happening.

HE SLAMMED THE DOOR SHUT, BUT IT WAS TOO LATE: THE WORLD WOULD SUFFER ILLNESS FOR ⚬NGONDA AND CHEBE'S⚬ TERRIBLE GREED.

THE STORY OF

Bat

— and —

Sun

FROM THE BEBA PEOPLE OF CAMEROON

A long time ago, Aleleb the Bat and Neneb the Sun were best friends. They were closer than heart and lungs, closer than earth and grave. Nearly every morning, one would fly over the ocean to visit the other until it was time for Neneb the Sun to start his descent below the horizon, when the two friends would be forced to wait until the next day to see each other again. For Neneb the Sun had a duty to the world to rise every morning and set every night, while Aleleb the Bat could come and go as he pleased. Besides their sizes, this was the only difference between the best friends.

Aleleb and Neneb most enjoyed looking down and marveling at the wondrous world together.

"Neneb, look in the dense trees of the forest: it's a nest full of newborn sunbirds, and their rainbow-colored mama is feeding them breakfast!" exclaimed Aleleb.

"Oh yes, beautiful!" replied Neneb, who then pointed with a long ray of sunlight. "Now look over there, over the deep, majestic sea! See how the waves crash as if they're dancing just for us!"

The two soared over the glittering ocean, each sighing at the beauty and vastness of the seascape.

"What a sight," Aleleb said, settling his wings and nestling close to his friend when they landed.

"A sweet sight is always sweeter when shared with a good friend," Neneb replied.

One day, after playing all morning with Neneb, Aleleb went home to his cave and found that his mother was very sick. How could this have happened?! He knew his mother to be stronger than the tall-est, most solid tree in the forest. She always took great care and com-forted him when he was frightened. She also ruled firmly over the family, doling out punishment and praise when neces-sary. But now, her body was weary. Now, she was hurting and could barely even speak. Aleleb had

Mediterranean
Sea

NORTHERN
AFRICA

Red
Sea

WESTERN
AFRICA

CENTRAL
AFRICA

EASTERN
AFRICA

ATLANTIC
OCEAN

SOUTHERN
AFRICA

never seen his mother like this before and he was greatly alarmed.

"I must get help for her!" he resolved. His little wings flew him as quickly as possible from one healer to another, and he begged them for their help. Some healers gave his sick mother medicinal herbs to drink. They gave offerings to their ancestors, chanting and pleading with them to heal Aleleb's mother. They did everything they could, but still his mother grew worse.

Finally, she said through gasps of breath, "My son, there is no more to be done. It seems now my time has come to join our ancestors." Aleleb began to cry, and his mother hushed him. "You have been so good to me, my son, and our life together as a family has been all I could have wished for. Do not grieve after I am gone, for I will be happy and safe with our ancestors and will always watch over you." She embraced her son as she fell asleep for the last time.

ALELEB LET OUT
A TERRIBLE CRY
SO LOUD IT MUST HAVE REACHED THE HEAVENS.

He did not know what to do with his grief-stricken heart. Tears streamed from him in torrents, as if they could wash away the sadness and pain. How would he ever live without his mother?

But finally, Aleleb stopped crying for a moment and decided what he had to do. It was a great honor to be buried on the day of one's death, so he would bury his mother before sunset. It would be tough, as it was already late in the afternoon and very close to dusk, but he knew that his best friend, Neneb, would surely help him.

Certainly Sun would wait for a just few extra moments before he dipped below the horizon so Bat could bury his mother before nightfall. After all, the two were closer than heart and lungs, closer than earth and grave.

Aleleb flew up to Neneb and said, "Neneb, my beloved mother has just died and joined our ancestors. I am beside myself with sadness, but I know I must honor my mother by burying her while there is still daylight. I beg you, my best friend, for one favor: for this day only, please let your light shine a little longer so I may commemorate the life and soul of my one and only mother. I must do my duty to her."

Neneb darkened. He replied slowly and sadly, "Aleleb, my dear friend, I am so sorry about your mother. I cannot imagine such a loss. But it doesn't work that way. I cannot hang in the sky and wait for you to bury your mother today. I must do my duty, too, and bring myself into the shadows at the appropriate time of day. The world depends on me."

Aleleb staggered backward as if he had been slapped in the face. His fur rose along the backs of his wings as he bristled at the thought of his best friend abandoning him in his moment of true need. Neneb could not even move one ray of sunlight for him! He would not even try to stretch the day one minute longer!

"How dare you!" Aleleb fumed, now devastated for the second time in one day. "What kind of friend are you?" He flew into the twilight, leaving Neneb to finish the day. With each flap of his wings, Aleleb grew angrier with Neneb and sadder with thoughts of his mother. It was a dreadful combination of feelings.

Aleleb arrived home as darkness crept over the land, and hastily buried his mother. By the time he finished the heavy task, the night was very dark already. As expected, he had not been able to honor his mother as he wished, and he bent his small body over his mother's fresh grave.

Aleleb gave over to sobs once again. He had lost two best friends in one day: his dear mother and that traitor, Neneb! Aleleb raged with grief and anger in his heart. *The next morning might as well not come, for all I care,* he thought. *I will never look upon Neneb's shining face again. I will never go visit him again. Never!* And he tucked himself into the darkest corner of his cave.

AND THAT IS WHY,
FROM THAT DAY FORWARD,

BATS AVOID THE SUN

AND ONLY LEAVE THEIR
DARK CAVES AT NIGHT.

Anansi
and the
Box of Stories

One clear and beautiful night, when the stars shone like punctures in the fabric of the dark sky, Anansi the Spider sat in his web up in a tree. He was enjoying himself immensely, looking down on a group of villagers sitting around a roaring fire. But the villagers didn't seem to be enjoying themselves as much as he.

"I'm bored," said one of the villagers, yawning.

"There's nothing to do," said another, staring blankly into the distance.

"Just another ordinary night around the fire," a woman said, rolling her eyes.

Bored, on a glorious night like tonight? Anansi thought. *How can I help?* Anansi the Spider loved a bit of fun and was saddened to see the people so spiritless.

Then, clear as the sky, the perfect solution appeared: Anansi would retrieve the box of stories for them! Then they'd be entertained and delighted.

You see, all the world's stories were kept locked in a big wooden box by the sky god, Nyame. Famous stories! Funny stories! Frightening stories! Nyame kept every single story dating back to the beginning of time, so the box contained the ancestral tales of any person or animal who had ever lived. The people around the fire would be absolutely delighted!

But how could he get that box of stories? Now, Anansi the Spider was a trickster of the highest order. He could deceive almost anybody into doing almost anything. Anansi talked the toad out of eating him more than once. He had conned the centipede out of eight of his most comfortable slippers. And most often he coerced flies into his web by telling them jokes. He even got around by hitching rides on the backs of people— some of the most spider-fearing creatures of all. Yes, Anansi was clever. But Nyame was a god, and too smart to be tricked into giving him that precious box. Still, Anansi loved a challenge as much as he loved a bit of fun.

The next morning, Anansi spun a silken thread long and strong enough to lead him up into the sky,

Mediterranean
Sea

Red
Sea

NORTHERN
AFRICA

CENTRAL
AFRICA

EASTERN
AFRICA

SOUTHERN
AFRICA

ATLANTIC
OCEAN

where Nyame lived. With the help of the gentle breeze, Anansi arrived at Nyame's heavenly home.

Bowing to the god on his eight little legs, Anansi said, "Great sky god, Nyame! What must I do to acquire your box of stories? I want to bring them to the people of Earth to enjoy."

Nyame laughed so hard, the sky shook. His voice boomed with thunder. "How do you propose to afford my box of stories, little spider? Kings have tried to buy my box, but even their riches were not enough to pay the price. Great warriors have tried to steal it, but they have never been able to wrest it from me."

Anansi asked again what he must do to get the stories. Nyame thought for a moment, a sneaky smile creeping up the corners of his mouth. He said, "Bring me these four things: **Onini the Python,** who can swallow a goat whole; **Osebo the Leopard,** with his spear-sharp teeth; **Mmoboro the Hornet,** whose sting feels like red-hot needles; and **Mmoatia the Invisible Fairy,** with the most terrible temper."

Anansi was frightened. Any one of these four creatures could easily kill him. He couldn't trick his way through this impossible task. But still, he wanted the people to have their stories.

"I promise to return with the creatures you desire!" he exclaimed with false confidence.

—— FIRST UP ——
ONINI THE PYTHON!
. . . .

To try and capture this snake as big as a tree trunk, Anansi went down to the watering hole where Onini drank.

"My oh my!" said Anansi, in a mocking tone, while scurrying back and forth along the bank of the watering hole. "You're a pretty big python, Onini. But I don't think you're nearly as long as this stick I have here . . ." Anansi feigned a confident posture atop a large stick on the ground.

Onini flicked his diamond-shaped head in the direction of the tiny voice that taunted him. Who would dare say such things to the snake who could swallow a goat whole? The python unfurled his hefty body slowly and deliberately, displaying every colorful scale, and glided right up to the spider. His giant grin bared knife-like fangs. Anansi looked up at Onini and suppressed the shiver running through all eight of his legs, but he did not flinch.

"Indeed, I am every bit as long as your stick, you puny spider. In fact, I'm bigger!" Onini the Python replied, incredulous. And to prove that he was longer than the stick, he lay down next to it, stretching out his body for what seemed like miles to Anansi.

"No, no, no," said Anansi, trying his luck. "You're not lying down straight enough. We can't truly measure your impressive length unless I attach you to the stick." Onini reluctantly agreed, and Anansi quickly bound the python to the stick with his web. The massive snake thrashed against the sticky web, which did not budge but became tighter with every movement.

"You're mine now!" Anansi celebrated. And the spider took Onini the Python, who could swallow a goat whole, up to Nyame in the sky.

Nyame was surprised to see the spider dragging the great Onini to his doorstep. *No matter,* thought Nyame. *Let's see him try to catch the Leopard!*

— NEXT —

OSEBO THE LEOPARD.

· · · · · · · · · · · ·

Anansi was terrified of this killing machine—with his powerful jaws and body that could easily crush a spider—so he had to be extra tricky and extra clever. Anansi knew that the fearsome Osebo walked the same route to the watering hole every night. So during the day Anansi dug a deep pit in the ground along the well-trodden path and covered it with sticks and leaves. It was completely hidden from sight. When Osebo strode to the water hole that night, he fell right in!

"Help! I'm trapped! Somebody, please help me . . ." the Leopard begged as he hopelessly flailed and lunged about the pit. Anansi could see and hear Osebo's long tail whipping through the air, and he approached the hole with great care.

"I can help you, Osebo," Anansi called as he threw long, silken threads of web down to him. "Wrap these around yourself like ropes, and I will pull you out."

Osebo was so thirsty he would have done anything to get out of the pit. So, he wrapped himself in Anansi's sticky web. Osebo soon realized he'd been tricked, because with each twist of web, the leopard became more entangled and more afraid. He strained his muscular body within the spider's silk wrapping.

When Anansi pulled Osebo out, the great creature could hardly move. The spider bound him even tighter.

"You're mine now!" Anansi celebrated. And the spider took Osebo the Leopard, with spear-sharp teeth, up to Nyame in the sky.

Nyame was shocked when he spotted Anansi hauling Osebo through the air. *I cannot believe it,* thought Nyame as Anansi delivered the mighty leopard. *Well, that's only two out of four. Surely Anansi will soon run out of his clever tricks.*

THIRD

MMOBORO *THE HORNET*.

· · · · · · · · · · ·

Now, carrying a calabash—a hollowed-out gourd—filled with water, Anansi went to the forest where Mmoboro the Hornet lived. Fearful of this creature's red-hot sting, he devised a plan to capture him. Anansi climbed to a branch just above the hornet's nest and poured some of the water onto a banana leaf above his own head. He then poured some water on the hornet's nest and shouted to Mmoboro, "It's raining very hard!"

The hornet peered out of his nest, droning loudly. Anansi couldn't tell what the sound meant. Was Mmoboro curious or annoyed? Was he alerting scores of fellow hornets, waiting to mobilize them with a single buzz?

"Your nest is getting wet," Anansi added. "Quick, fly into my calabash! It will keep you dry."

Mmoboro, seeing all the dripping water, flew quick-as-a-flash toward the calabash—but the sight of

Mmoboro's stinger sent shocks through Anansi. The spider flinched, causing the hornet to miss the gourd and bump his head on the rim. Mmoboro staggered backward and Anansi gasped. *Oh no!* he thought. *I've missed my chance!*

"What is this trick?" Mmoboro buzzed angrily. "Let me in!" Anansi tilted the calabash's opening toward the hornet, and prayed he'd make it inside this time. Mmoboro landed at the bottom of the calabash—success! Anansi quickly covered the opening with the banana leaf and wrapped his sticky web around the whole thing.

Mmoboro was trapped . . . and he was furious! Anansi heard him sounding a pattern of buzzes: long-short-short-long, long-short-short-long. He was alerting the others in his nest! With no time to celebrate, Anansi glided away quickly on the breeze, and up, up, up toward Nyame in the sky. Mmoboro was safely in tow, and the rest of the swarm was far behind.

Nyame saw Anansi gliding along the breeze with a wrapped calabash held firmly in his eight legs. "Here!" Anansi said, out of breath, dropping the calabash at Nyame's feet. "Inside this calabash is Mmoboro the Hornet, whose sting feels like red-hot needles!" Anansi glided off to capture the last of the four, leaving Nyame slack-jawed at his own doorstep. At this point, the sky god thought to hide his box of stories. But a promise was a promise, and there was still one more chance for Anansi to foul up.

AND LASTLY
MMOATIA THE INVISIBLE FAIRY.

Anansi knew that catching the Invisible Fairy would be the hardest task of all . . . and one of the most dangerous. When she got angry—and that was often—she could kill any living thing with just a touch of her finger. She could throw lightning from her eyes and set whole forests on fire. Her screech could cause small creatures like Anansi to disintegrate at once.

And Anansi couldn't even see her, so how could he capture her?! He knew he had to make her—or her terrible temper—visible somehow. So the clever trickster created a little doll out of twigs and leaves and pieces of fluff, and smeared sticky sap all over it. The doll was exactly the same size as Mmoatia the Invisible Fairy, and looked sweet and friendly. He brought the doll to the thicket where fairies were known to play, placed it against a tree, and set a bowl of delicious yams in front of it. Then Anansi scurried onto a low branch nearby to wait.

And sure enough, Mmoatia the Invisible Fairy eventually arrived that evening when the moon was high in the sky. She ate the delicious yams and sighed a satisfied sigh, thanking the doll. But when the doll said nothing in return, Mmoatia's temper began to bubble and boil.

"You're incredibly rude!" she shouted at the doll, then slapped it with both hands. Nothing happened to the doll, of course, but Mmoatia's fingers stuck to the sticky sap. "Let me go, or I'll kick you!" the fairy shouted.

Struggling with the doll, Mmoatia kicked with both her invisible feet and they got stuck, too. While Anansi still couldn't see the fairy, he could see the doll being tossed everywhere. From the safety of his low branch, he giggled at his cleverness, thinking of the box of stories that was soon to be his. But Anansi knew he had to act quickly, as Mmoatia's temper was growing.

The fairy thrashed about on the ground, trying to unstick herself from the doll. But with each punch and jerk of her body, Mmoatia became more trapped. Anansi had to be very careful not to get crushed, so he waited for a lull in the action. Then he swiftly picked up the doll and the invisible fairy, and wrapped his web many times around them both.

Mmoatia tried to lash out and unleashed a bolt of lightning from her eyes, which hit a tree and set it on fire. Soon the whole fairy thicket was crackling in flames. Anansi scurried left and right, holding onto the doll and the fairy while dodging burning branches falling from the trees. The heat was near unbearable for the little spider, and Mmoatia's cackle sounded in his ears, making him stagger. Anansi managed to throw a silken thread in the direction of the upward wind. The silk caught the strong breeze and floated the spider, the doll, and the tempestuous fairy up and away.

"You're mine now!" Anansi celebrated as they cleared the burning forest. And the spider brought Mmoatia the Invisible Fairy, with the most terrible temper, up to Nyame in the sky.

Anansi had done it! He'd captured Onini the Python, Osebo the Leopard, Mmoboro the Hornet, and Mmoatia the Invisible Fairy . . . all for Nyame the Sky God. The wooden box of stories would soon be his to deliver to the people!

When Anansi arrived at the doorstep with the fourth and final creature, Nyame was defeated—but impressed. The sky god bowed his head for the very first time. Anansi bowed back, grateful for the challenge and glorying in his success.

"Little, clever spider," Nyame said to Anansi, "you have done what many great kings and warriors have not been able to. As promised, and with many blessings, I grant you my wooden box of stories!"

As Anansi released the stories, the world began to take on a more vibrant color, which intensified the more the stories were told and retold. The wind laughed, the animals cheered, and the people listened to the stories and loved them. The stories entertained, delighted, and deepened their lives, just as Anansi had hoped. The people told the stories to their children, and their children told the stories to their children, and so on, passing them down for generations.

. . . .

AND THIS IS HOW YOU ARE ABLE TO HEAR THE TALE OF "ANANSI AND THE BOX OF STORIES," —— **EVEN TODAY.** ——

MYTHS OF
... ## EUROPE

From tales of strange creatures to legendary warriors and gods, these myths are lively and adventurous, evoking a rich culture of storytelling from ancient times to present day. Many of these stories were meant to caution the reader against greed, trickery, and danger. Enter the world of European myths, if you dare. . . .

ATLANTIC
OCEAN

*Norwegian
Sea*

**NORTHERN
EUROPE**

*North
Sea*

**EASTERN
EUROPE**

*Celtic
Sea*

**WESTERN
EUROPE**

**SOUTH-
EASTERN
EUROPE**

Black Sea

Aegean Sea

*Mediterranean
Sea*

The Selkies

FROM SCOTTISH MYTHOLOGY

There once was a fisherman who lived on a small island in northern Scotland, where the mist hung low and the land was so green that there was not even a name for the color. The fisherman was poor, but his heart and mind were married to the sea. So long as he was among the waves, he felt at peace.

The fisherman would spend all day on his small boat, but usually did not catch many fish. Perhaps he was destined to be unlucky. He had no wife or children, which he greatly desired.

One day, as the sun set on another meager catch, the fisherman docked his little boat. As he began looping the coarse rope to a post on shore, something made him stop. It was a voice. No—it was many voices, all singing a lyrical tune together, harmonizing like angels.

The light was getting low, so the fisherman strained his eyes and peered around his little rough patch of rock, following the voices. His eyes finally focused on the source, and he blinked once, twice, thrice—not believing what he was seeing.

ON THE JAGGED OUTCROPPING RIGHT OUTSIDE HIS SMALL COTTAGE, WERE A HALF-DOZEN

SELKIES.

They lounged and gazed out at the sea, while singing the most exquisite song that ever was.

The fisherman had heard folktales about the Selkie people since he was a little boy. They were enigmatic creatures and shape-shifters, able to live as seals in the ocean or shed their skins on land and exist as men and women. He could tell they were Selkies not only from the seal skins strewn about the rocks, but also because they were extraordinarily beautiful. They glowed like quartz in the twilight, their hair was like hot flames licking the air all around them, and their eyes . . . Well, they were a color of green that the fisherman could not find the name for.

What a rare sight! the fisherman thought, delighted. He stood back

from the group to watch, mesmerized. The Selkies finished their song and began playing and giggling—a sound that was like bubbles fizzing and popping. The fisherman smiled at the spirited scene and couldn't help but laugh along.

Then there was one Selkie who held his interest the most. He suddenly noticed that he was no longer looking at the entire group, but his eyes were now trained upon her alone. The fisherman thought he locked eyes with hers for a moment, and he abruptly stood up and began moving toward the group.

"Hello!" he called to her. "What's your name?"

The fisherman stumbled forward, drawn to the Selkies' magic and unaware of himself. But when they saw the fisherman, they were spooked. They slipped back into their seal skins and quickly dove into the sea, disappearing beneath the lapping waves.

The fisherman walked out onto the rocks where the magical Selkies had been playing just moments ago. *What is that?* he thought as he bent down and picked up something lying on the rocks. It was a Selkie skin—smooth and sleek—and here it was still on shore!

What luck! Now the fisherman could bring the Selkie skin into town and tell everyone his story. "Surely, they'll believe me if I show them this!" he said, throwing the skin around his wide shoulders. "Maybe I can even sell it and make a bit of money," the poor fisherman guessed.

But as he turned toward his cottage, he heard another sound, much sadder than the singing he had heard just moments ago. It was the beautiful young Selkie he had had his eyes

on earlier, but she was curled up on the rock and weeping. The fisherman could barely stand the sadness.

"Oh dear. Why are you crying?" the fisherman asked, his heart now pounding in his chest. The young woman leaned back as he approached her, and he stopped in his tracks.

"Sir, that seal skin you are holding— that is mine. I am a Selkie, and I need it in order to return to the sea. Without it, I cannot go home," she said, and she began weeping fresh tears again.

But the fisherman knew that he could not give it back, for now he was madly in love with her. This was his chance to keep her with him forever, since the one who holds a Selkie's skin also holds power over her. He gripped the precious skin tighter around him.

He sat down on the rocks just a few feet away, not wanting to frighten her any more than she already was. He spoke gently to her, almost in a whisper, almost as if he couldn't believe it himself. "Sweet Selkie, I cannot possibly give you back your seal skin because you are the most precious thing I've ever encountered. I must keep you with me. Please be my wife, and I promise I will make you happy." The fisherman knew she couldn't say no as long as he held her seal skin. The prospect of their life together made him feel elated.

Her eyes cast downward to the sea. "Sir, you know I must stay on land with you as long as you have my skin. I will do as you request, but know that I can never be happy here. The sea is my home and that is where I belong."

The fisherman took her delicate hand in his and led her to his warm cottage. This was the first time he touched the Selkie, and it felt like tiny bubbles fizzing and popping in his blood.

At first there was a nagging feeling in the fisherman's heart that she might steal back her seal skin and leave him at any time. So he took to bringing it everywhere. He wore it like a cape around his shoulders, not minding the constant weight as long as it meant she would stay with him.

The fisherman truly did love his wife and took great care to ensure she was happy. After a while, they settled into their life together. He was generous with what little he had and was always kind and gentle with her. Each morning, he would bring her coffee in bed and rub life into her cold feet. He always told her he loved her, and kissed her face last thing before leaving and first thing when coming home. After a long day out on his boat, the fisherman brought her shells and strands of seaweed, anything to remind her of home. She used them to decorate their small cottage.

It seemed as though she had found a way to be content on land. Each night, before they fell asleep, she would sing him the lyrical song he had heard on the day they first met. This was the way he knew she loved him back, and it filled him with a calm, sublime joy.

As time passed, the fisherman forgot his fear that his Selkie would leave him and he stopped wearing her skin around his neck. But still he could not risk her taking it back, so he hid the skin in a secret place where he knew she would never look.

Soon the couple grew into a trio, as they welcomed their first child. Then their second, then their third, and so on. The Selkie and the fisherman had seven beautiful human sons and daughters together, creating a loving, laughing family in their small cottage. Their lives and hearts were full.

When the fisherman was not working out on his boat, the young family would play together on the beach. While the children would run and skip and collect stones, their mother would sit by the shore, the waves rolling right up to her toes.

"Mother, you look sad. What is the matter?" one of her children sat beside her and asked.

"It is nothing, my sweet child," she replied. "I only love the sea too much." With this, she gave her son a squeeze, as if to reassure him that she loved him more. But still, she looked wistfully at the gentle waves and shed a single, secret tear.

Several years later, the fisherman started taking his children with him to collect the daily catch. Six of them were now grown enough to work, and the fisherman could use all the help he could get. The youngest one was to stay back with his mother.

One morning, they all donned their rubber boots and coats and packed lunches, for they would be gone until the afternoon. The fisherman and his oldest sons and daughters all kissed Mother and their little brother on their way out the door.

The youngest son waved enthusiastically from the doorframe. Standing beside his mother, he watched as his father and his six siblings pushed off the dock and out to sea for the day. The mist hung low over the placid water, and the little boat grew smaller as it raced away.

Mother's eyes misted over, too, as she gazed out onto the sea that she still loved so. She thought she spied a pod of seals out in the distance. For the first time in a long while, the Selkie allowed herself to cry as she thought about her old life. Soon she was sobbing at the entryway to their cottage.

Her son looked up at his mother quizzically. He had never seen her like this before, and he was shaken by the sight. "Mother, why are you crying?"

The Selkie spilled the secrets of her past to her child, before she realized what she was doing. "I am crying, my child, because I am very sad. I was once a sea creature—a seal, actually. The sea is my true home, and I can never return to it."

"Is that why there's a seal skin hidden behind one of the rafters?" the boy asked innocently.

"What did you say?" His mother stopped crying instantly. She took her boy by the hand, and together they walked back into their family cottage. Wordlessly, the boy climbed up the bookcase, reached his hand into a small, dark space, and pulled out the luxuriant seal skin. He gave it to his mother and she caressed it carefully. It was in the exact same condition as when she had last seen it many years

ago. She looked at her darling son with a mixture of elation and grief.

"One day I was alone in the house with Father. He thought I was napping, and I saw him clutching this to his chest," the boy told her, even though she hadn't asked. "When he noticed I had appeared, Father quickly stuffed it back into the spot I just took it from. We never said a word to each other about it.

"I thought it must be some kind of treasure. Now I know: it is your seal skin."

The Selkie couldn't believe what she was holding, and how distant the prospect of returning to the sea had been just moments ago. Now it was in her hands. She held her precious seal skin close to her chest and looked down at her sweet boy.

Then the Selkie pulled her son very close to her. They embraced for a long time, the mother kissing her son's face and hugging his tiny frame. She made sure to imprint his sweet, child-like scent in her nose and remember what his soft hair felt like. The boy did not try to pull away as normally he might, although he did not know this would be the last time he saw his mother.

"My sweet boy, I will always love you and your siblings. Please tell them I will keep you all in my heart . . ." Then the Selkie picked up her seal skin and ran out the door. The last thing the boy saw was his mother's flippers as she dove into the sea.

During lunchtime, the fisherman pointed out a beautiful, sleek group of seals that swam by their boat.

"Look, children!" he said, and pointed toward the water. "What a magnificent creature the seal is." The children all nodded and stopped their chewing to watch the seals pass.

One of the seals stopped, its head turning toward the boat as if to have a good look at the children and the man. Its eyes were a rare color of green, and the fisherman thought he recognized them from somewhere.

"Time to head home, children!" the fisherman called, shaking the strange thought from his mind. He began rowing away. The seal cried out one last time before she disappeared under the water, but they were now too far in the distance to hear it.

ONLY LATER WOULD THE **FISHERMAN REALIZE: TO IMPRISON** —o THE ONE YOU LOVE IS o— **NOT LOVE AT ALL.**

The Fisherman and His Wife

FROM GERMAN FOLKLORE

Once upon a time, there was a poor fisherman who never had much luck at catching fish. Every day he went out to sea, thinking, *Today will be the day I catch something good,* and every day he came back to the run-down shack that he shared with his wife with not much to speak of.

One afternoon, he was out fishing on the clear, placid water, the sun shining down on his rugged face. The fisherman cast his line, hopeful as ever, and watched as it sank down deep to where he could no longer see it. After a few moments, something tugged the line! The fisherman reeled it up and saw at the end of his hook was a large flounder. He and his wife could dine for many nights on this beauty.

But then the fish began to speak! "Fisherman, please let me live," he said. "Do not take me home and eat me, for I am not your normal, everyday flounder but an enchanted prince. You must throw me back in the cool, calm sea."

ATLANTIC
OCEAN

Norwegian
Sea

NORTHERN
EUROPE

North
Sea

Celtic
Sea

EASTERN
EUROPE

WESTERN
EUROPE

SOUTH-
EASTERN
EUROPE

Black Sea

Aegean Sea

Mediterranean
Sea

How could the fisherman argue with a talking fish? Especially one who claimed to be a prince? He immediately tossed him back into the water and bid him well, as he swam back to the bottom of the sea.

As usual, the fisherman returned home that night to his run-down shack, empty-handed.

"Catch anything today?" his wife asked, hoping he had.

"Actually, I did catch something," the fisherman replied. "A flounder. But he spoke to me and told me he was an enchanted prince, so I threw him back in the sea."

"An enchanted prince! Did you request anything from him in return for sparing his life?" the fisherman's wife asked.

"No, I didn't think of it. Whatever should I have asked for?"

"Why, I would have asked this fish-prince for a cozy little cottage for us to live in. Our shack is freezing, and we could do with a nicer place. Go back to the sea and ask the flounder to give us a cottage. You've already spared his life—surely he will repay you in kind," the fisherman's wife said.

The man was a little embarrassed, asking a fish for a house. While the fisherman was poor, he was also still

proud, but he wanted to make his wife happy. If she wanted a cozy little cottage, he would go ask for one.

So he rowed his little boat out to the same spot, but the sea was no longer clear like it had been earlier that day. It was now the color of bile—yellow and green mixed together.

Still feeling unsettled about his request, the fisherman conjured the fish-prince by chanting:

RISE UP, UP, UP, MY LITTLE FISH,
AND ASK ME, ASK ME, WHAT I WISH!
MY WIFE HAS WANTS, MY WIFE HAS NEEDS—
BRING IT TO US, IF YOU PLEASE?

The flounder swam to the surface and asked the fisherman, "What does your wife want?"

"Good evening, fish. If I may be so bold to ask you ... Well, my wife says that after I caught you today ... you see," the fisherman stuttered, "she says that before I spared your life I should have asked you for something in return. My wife is tired of living in a dirty old shack and would like a cozy little cottage."

"Go back home and you will see she already has what she wants," said the flounder.

And indeed, when the fisherman returned home he saw his wife standing on the front porch of a perfect little cottage. She was smiling, and she took him by the hand to give him the tour of their new place.

"Here's the little front garden filled with sweet lavender ... and come in through our front door to the parlor. Look, there's even a fireplace! And our bedroom has a view of the sea from the four-poster bed," she rattled off. The fisherman touched the soft bed

linens and couldn't believe it. "And here is the dining room, and here is the kitchen with an icebox and everything ..." his wife continued, listing all the lovely features of the cottage.

"See, Husband? Isn't this much nicer than before?" she called out to him from the pantry.

Yes, in fact it was. Inside, everything was in its place, well-appointed and as comfortable as could be inside. And everything was charming outside, with a garden that wrapped around the entire house and burst with vegetables, fruits, and flowers. There were even chickens out back. The fisherman thought, *I could get used to this!*

"Yes," replied the fisherman to his wife. "This is very nice. We could be very happy here."

"Hmm ..." his wife said, scratching her chin. "Well, we'll see about that ..."

The couple had dinner in their gleaming kitchen, then went to sleep in their downy bed. The fisherman had never had such a good night of sleep in his life.

But after a couple of weeks, the fisherman's wife was getting restless. She would pace in the garden every morning, muttering to herself. Then she would come into the cottage and open cupboards and closets, sighing each time.

Over porridge one morning, she said to her husband, "I've been thinking, this cottage is too small for us. I can barely move around this kitchen, and we keep bumping into each other in the only bathroom in the house. There's nothing to be done with that tiny garden out there.

"I think the flounder could give us something bigger. Go back and ask him to give us a palace. That's where I want to live."

The fisherman blushed, already embarrassed by the thought of asking. "But Wife, this cottage is perfectly fine, and it's enough for the two of us. A palace would be too large. Why do you want a palace, my dear?"

"Why wouldn't I? Go and ask him for a palace. You've already saved his life. Surely this is not too much to ask."

So the fisherman went out to his boat again. His head was swimming with excuses not to go, as he was very reluctant to find the flounder again and ask him for an upgrade on the cottage, but he went anyway.

He rowed his little boat out to the same spot. Now the sea was no longer yellow and green—it was thick and dark purplish-blue, like a fresh bruise.

The fisherman chanted:

RISE UP, UP, UP, MY LITTLE FISH,
AND ASK ME, ASK ME, WHAT I WISH!
MY WIFE HAS WANTS, MY WIFE HAS NEEDS—
BRING IT TO US, IF YOU PLEASE?

The flounder swam to the surface and asked, "What does your wife want?"

The fisherman began. "My wife wishes to have a palace now—"

"Go back home and you will see she already has what she wants," said the flounder.

When the fisherman returned home, he almost passed right by!

"Hellooooooo!" his wife called from the top of a wide marble staircase leading up to a grand stone palace. She was beaming from ear to ear, and it pleased the fisherman to see his wife so happy. Like when he had first arrived at the cottage, his wife took him by the hand and led him through their new home. But this time, there were butlers and grand halls, silken sofas and crystal chandeliers, tables overflowing with food and gardens teeming with roses—all the luxuries one could imagine, and amazing views across the valleys, hills, and surrounding towns.

And just like with the cottage, his wife soon tired of it and asked for more.

"Husband, look at all of this," she said, admiring the view. "Couldn't we be king and queen, and rule over this land? Go ask the fish to make us royalty." The fisherman admitted that he liked the idea of being called king.

So he went out to his boat again and rowed to the very same spot. Now the sea was no longer dark purple-blue, like a bruise. Instead it was roiling and bubbling with a foul stench, which felt like a punch in the face.

The fisherman covered his nose and chanted:

RISE UP, UP, UP, MY LITTLE FISH,
AND ASK ME, ASK ME, WHAT I WISH!
MY WIFE HAS WANTS, MY WIFE HAS NEEDS—
BRING IT TO US, IF YOU PLEASE?

The flounder swam to the surface and asked, "What do you want?"

"We wish to be king and queen," the fisherman said.

"Go back home. Your wife is already queen, and you will be king once you arrive," said the flounder.

The fisherman went home and found it was now a castle, ten times the size of his palace! It was all there: turrets and flags waving in the breeze and a moat! The fisherman, who was now a king, sauntered through the arched entrance of the castle. *His* castle. The trumpets blared as he entered, and the court knelt at his feet.

"Where is my queen?" he asked. At once, the doors to a great hall opened wide, revealing a crowd of lords and ladies, dukes and duchesses, servants and jesters. In front of them all, his wife—the queen—sat on a golden throne flecked with diamonds and rubies. She was draped in red velvet and purple satin, and wore a heavy, jeweled crown. On each one of her fingers she wore a different, dazzling ring.

Next to her throne was an empty one. The queen gestured for him to sit.

"We are now king and queen," he said once he had taken his place by her side. "Now we will want for nothing!"

"Not true, my dear king," she said. "We could want to become emperor and empress, we two. Couldn't we?"

"Could we?" he replied. And at once, the king leaped from his throne and went out to his boat again.

This time, it was difficult rowing to the same spot to meet the flounder, for the seas were thick and black like molasses. The current bubbled up from below, and it was hot as a boiling pot of water.

The fisherman wiped his brow and chanted:

RISE UP, UP, UP, MY LITTLE FISH,
AND ASK ME, ASK ME, WHAT I WISH!
MY WIFE HAS WANTS, MY WIFE HAS NEEDS—
BRING IT TO US, IF YOU PLEASE?

The flounder swam to the surface and asked, "What do you want now?"

"Make us emperor and empress," the fisherman demanded.

"Go home. You are already emperor and empress," said the flounder.

When he returned, he barged into the great hall where his wife was sitting on a throne two miles high. She wore a crown that engulfed her

entire head down to her neck. Her ladies-in-waiting, who were floating all around her, lifted the crown off her head, so she could see her husband.

"We are emperor and empress now!" she called down to him.

"I want to be a pope!" he called up to her. She smiled and her eyes went wild.

"Yes," she said. "Yes, we shall be popes!"

The fisherman turned on his heels and headed back to his little boat. The wind gusted all around him, and the clouds hung low as evening closed in, making it nearly impossible to get out to sea, but he climbed aboard his rowboat and pushed out. Immediately, great waves sent his little boat back to shore. He set out

again, and again angry waves tossed him back. The sky turned red and threatening. But the man persisted, and made it through dense, dark waters to the spot where he usually found the flounder.

The fisherman cowered as a bolt of lightning crashed nearby, and chanted:

RISE UP, UP, UP, MY LITTLE FISH,
AND ASK ME, ASK ME, WHAT I WISH!
MY WIFE HAS WANTS, MY WIFE HAS NEEDS—
BRING IT TO US, IF YOU PLEASE?

"What do you want?"
"To be a pope!"

○—●—"GO HOME. —●—○
YOU ARE BOTH NOW
POPES",
SAID THE FLOUNDER.

The man went home.
It was not a home any
longer, but an enormous
cathedral surrounded
by castles, palaces, cot-
tages, and shacks.

A massive crowd of people, from very rich to very poor, very old to very young, gathered around outside the church. They were all waiting to catch a glimpse of their new popes. Some of the people were crying. Some were covering their faces in prayer.

The fisherman marched forward as the crowd parted for him. He couldn't wait to find his wife and say,

SEE! SEE WHAT I HAVE DONE FOR US!

The fisherman found his way to the holy chamber, which was illuminated by hundreds of sparkling lanterns. He could barely see through so much blinding light. He glanced all around at the stained-glass windows, which depicted his and his wife's rise from humble beginnings to the holiest seat in the entire world. Through the center of the chamber, a line of people snaked out the door. At the head of it all sat the fisherman's wife, now a pope.

She was clothed in iridescent gold and silver robes, which shimmered like divine spirits. Her head boasted a three-tiered crown, dripping with diamonds more brilliant than the thousand lanterns that surrounded her. With a golden scepter firmly in one hand, she held out her other hand so that kings, queens, and emperors could kiss her many rings.

"We are now popes," she said as she nodded to him. Several attendants surrounded the fisherman and adorned him with attire similar to his wife's. The kings, queens, and emperors now kneeled before him and kissed his rings, too.

"Yes, we are now popes," he replied, distracted as he watched the sun set behind her in a gaudy display of colors. The moon was already high in the sky. The pope twitched and looked down at his decorated fingers. Then he raised his hands above his head, framing the moon between them.

"But, my dear, we could become even more…" He now desired to control the sun and moon, the Earth and its heavens.

The fisherman ran off at once,

raving at the sky like a maniac. The green sky raged back at him, sending torrents of rain upon his three-tiered crown and drenching his iridescent robes. As he ran past castles and palaces, houses and shacks to get down to the shore, the storm picked up, knocking over trees and blowing the tops off buildings. Lightning bolted downward and cracked mountains in half, sending gigantic rocks plummeting into the sea.

From the shore, the fisherman took off in his little boat into waves the size of killer whales. Over and over again, his boat tossed violently through the surges. Nevertheless, he arrived at the same spot where the flounder always came up to give him what he and his wife wanted.

The fisherman yelled at the deep, fuming sea:

RISE UP, UP, UP, MY LITTLE FISH,
AND ASK ME, ASK ME, WHAT I WISH!
MY WIFE HAS WANTS, MY WIFE HAS NEEDS—
BRING IT TO US, IF YOU PLEASE?

The flounder rose up and bounced on the surface. His bulging, filmy eyes stared at the fisherman. "What?!" he said.

"My wife and I want to be gods!"

"You've asked for too much! Go home. Your wife is sitting in your run-down shack again."

The fisherman returned to shore, then slowly walked back to his first home, the tiny shack. He couldn't believe he had lost everything. But the fisherman and his wife had become consumed by riches, power, and greed. Now they were left with nothing again.

When the fisherman arrived at the filthy, freezing shack, he found his wife inside quietly weeping.

HE WRAPPED HIS ARMS AROUND HER, AND THE GREEDY COUPLE RESUMED THEIR POOR LIFE.

Athena, Arachne,
and the
Dueling Looms

FROM GREEK MYTHOLOGY

In the Greek kingdom of Lydia, east of the islands dotting the aquamarine Aegean Sea, lived a maiden named Arachne. She was just a shepherd's daughter. Not much was special about Arachne—besides her exceptional weaving.

Arachne was so skilled at her loom, it was almost as if her talent were supernatural. Everyone in her small village would come to see her begin her daily projects. "What will Arachne weave today?" they would wonder before they set off on their own daily tasks. Then again each evening, people would crowd outside her door to admire her day's handiwork. Wood nymphs and fairies would gather around the loom to watch her weave beautiful art, from tapestries to linens. Arachne's hands worked like needle-beaked birds, threading and plucking and embroidering all day long: a fine pattern here, a perfect color there.

Word of Arachne's immense skill

traveled far beyond the borders of Lydia, and she soon became known as the premier artisan of thread and cloth. Some even said she had skills to match the gods . . .

The goddess Athena, nestled in her home on Mount Olympus, tried to ignore the expert weavings of this annoying young girl. After all, Athena was the goddess of handicraft, particularly weaving. She controlled who was and was not bestowed with this special gift of creativity. But had the arrogant Arachne ever once paid homage to the goddess who showered her with skill? No! Athena pushed the thought away.

But one day, Athena overheard the wood nymphs *oohing* and *ahhing* over another of Arachne's masterworks.

ATLANTIC OCEAN

Norwegian Sea

NORTHERN EUROPE

North Sea

Celtic Sea

WESTERN EUROPE

EASTERN EUROPE

SOUTH-EASTERN EUROPE

Black Sea

Aegean Sea

Mediterranean Sea

"Craftswoman Arachne," one of them sighed, "how did you learn to master the loom? And how do you dream up such ethereal designs?"

"I've taught myself," Arachne confessed. "And my designs come straight from my own heart."

"Surely Athena has something to do with your skill?" another wood nymph suggested. Arachne bristled at this.

"Surely Athena does not," she replied curtly. "I have never met the goddess in my life, nor have I ever felt her influence. My skill is mine and mine alone."

And that was it! Athena, infuriated by the girl's rude response, swooped down from Mount Olympus at once. But Athena was also

wise and fair; instead of unleashing her anger on the young maiden, she would allow Arachne to apologize.

Disguised as an old woman, Athena approached Arachne's front door, knocked, and interrupted her weaving.

"My dear," Athena said to Arachne, once inside her weaving studio, "as I

was passing just now, I overheard what you said about the goddess Athena. Indeed, you are talented at what you do. The cloths you weave are worthy of kings and queens. But, a young person—even one as skilled as yourself—should be wary of what she says. You must speak with respect about those gods who bestow such great skill upon mere mortals, lest the skill be taken away. I urge you to apologize to the goddess Athena for your insolent words."

"There is nothing to apologize for," Arachne replied. "I meant what I said. My art is mine and mine alone. No god or goddess can touch it. Let Athena try to test my talent!"

At once, Athena pulled off her tattered old-woman disguise and cast it to the ground.

THE PROUD GODDESS

NOW STOOD TWICE AS TALL AS A HUMAN, IN SHIMMERING ROBES, AND GLARED AT HER NEMESIS.

"HERE I AM, DREADFUL GIRL!" she shouted at Arachne. The wood nymphs in attendance all bowed to the great goddess before them. But

Arachne did not even flinch. Athena continued, "I challenge you to a weaving contest. King of the gods, Zeus, shall be our judge!"

— "I GLADLY ACCEPT — YOUR CHALLENGE."

ARACHNE BOLDLY REPLIED.

Zeus appeared beside his daughter Athena and produced two of the most expensive, well-crafted looms in the kingdom. The looms sat facing each other, right outside Arachne's humble home, so anyone who wanted to watch, could.

But Arachne refused Zeus's fancy loom; she preferred her own. And with that, she dragged it outside to face her divine opponent.

Zeus threw down a thunderbolt, signaling the start of the challenge. "May the best tapestry win!" he boomed.

Athena and Arachne got straight to work, heads down, furiously weaving away.

The goddess wasted no time and began weaving one of four images she had planned for her tapestry. Each one depicted a scene in which a human committed hubris, or extreme pride, thinking themselves equal to the gods. As Athena weaved her scenes, Arachne saw that these humans had been punished greatly, each punishment more gruesome and severe than the next. Athena's tapestry was meant to teach Arachne a lesson. But still, Arachne wove on.

The maiden's handiwork was marvelous. Her tapestry materialized from pure emotion, as if Arachne's heart truly did guide her weaving. Her fingers moved faster than ever, blurring with activity.

And as her tapestry emerged, so did the irreverent scenes it depicted. Arachne's weaving scorned the gods, portraying immortals abusing mortals, time after time. There were images of Hades trapping Persephone in the underworld, Hera turning women into monsters, and even

Athena challenging Arachne to this very weaving contest—with jealousy in the goddess's eyes. The corruption of all the gods was laid bare for all to see! Their faults, clearly displayed. No god was left untouched in Arachne's takedown—especially Zeus, king of the gods, whose treatment of mortals was despicable. Arachne wanted her tapestry to be a lesson to them, as well. With each stroke of her loom, Arachne looked up and smirked at Athena and Zeus, waiting for the wrath on their faces to turn to defeat. For it was clear: Arachne was the better weaver, hands down.

Finally, the last touches were finished, and the contest was over. Arachne, proud and exhausted, stood tall in front of her loom and allowed her adoring fans to view her handiwork. The buzz of the crowd went from whisper to roar as the people admired the most magnificent thing they had ever seen.

Athena's stare turned dead cold. Zeus's stare turned white hot. The combination was terrifying, but Arachne tried to dwell in the feeling of victory instead. For she *had* beaten Athena, the goddess of weaving.

ZEUS GRINNED AND SAID THROUGH CLENCHED TEETH, "THE WINNER IS . . . ATHENA!"

"What?!" said Arachne.

"What?!" said Arachne's crowd of admirers.

"Athena is the winner. And as punishment for your pride and arrogance, I decree that you, Arachne, may never touch another loom as long as you shall live!" Zeus dealt this final blow, and with his lightning bolt he sealed her fists shut.

She dropped to the floor, weeping and staring at her mangled hands. Without the use of her fingers, Arachne would never be able to create again.

"If I cannot weave, I will never be

whole," she wept. "My heart will never truly beat again if my art cannot continue."

Athena knew that Arachne's tapestry was better than hers. But how could it be so? No human could surpass a god! The goddess did not know where this mortal had come from, or how she had achieved her otherworldly talents. But Athena did know that there was one way to let Arachne continue making her art and also keep her away from the gods.

So Athena took pity on Arachne and turned Arachne into a spider. Arachne felt her eight arms now move as her ten fingers once did, to weave the exquisite silk. She fell into a calm, enchanting rhythm as she created something brand new.

AS ATHENA WALKED AWAY FROM HER WORTHY OPPONENT, SHE THOUGHT SHE SAW HUNDREDS OF TINY LETTER A's WOVEN INTO THE FABRIC OF ARACHNE'S FIRST WEB, SHIMMERING IN THE LATE-DAY SUN . . .

MYTHS OF
...
ASIA

The myths of Asia are steeped in reverence for mystical gods: some dangerous, some benevolent, and all powerful.

These stories bring the reader straight into the heart of various Asian cultures, values, and traditions. With dueling creation myths and the tale of an elephant-headed deity, these legends are legendary!

Ganesh

Lord Ganesh is the most important deity in Hinduism. He is the god of wisdom and success, and is known to impose or remove obstacles in people's lives. Therefore, Ganesh is always worshipped first, and before a person sets off on any important venture.

Ganesh is portrayed as a human with an elephant's head and four arms. The arms represent the four types of creatures on Earth: those that live on land, those that live in water, those that live both on land and in water, and those that live in the air. His mother is the goddess Parvati, and his father is Lord Shiva. This is the story of how Ganesh came to be.

One day, the four-armed goddess Parvati, ruler of fertility, love, and divine power, wanted some time to herself. She was exhausted, always answering others' calls for help and healing. The afternoon was overcast and dull, perfect weather for reclining with a book and a warm cup of tea.

After instructing Nandi—the bull belonging to her husband, Lord Shiva—to guard the door to her chambers so no one could come in, she settled in for an afternoon of quiet. Two of her four hands held the book, one held the cup of tea, and the other twirled her silken hair.

Nandi had been guarding the door in the hallway for only a few minutes when he heard Lord Shiva come home and shut the front door, take off his boots and coat, and mount the stairs to

the chambers. Nandi stood up straight and alert, ready to welcome his master.

"Good afternoon, sir," the bull said to Shiva.

"Good afternoon, Nandi. Please let me through, as I am tired and want to enter my chambers to rest," Shiva replied.

"But, Lord, I have been instructed by Parvati not to let anyone in, as she does not want to be disturbed."

"Nonsense! Let me through," Shiva said again, getting annoyed. "I am the omnipotent force of life, Lord Shiva! Your loyalties are to me, not to the goddess." He barged in past Nandi.

"What are you doing back already?" Parvati said to him, flustered. "I had just settled in to relax and did not want to be disturbed. Didn't Nandi tell you?"

"Nandi answers to me, not to you! I came in anyway," he spat out.

"Well, leave now," Parvati instructed. "I want to be alone." Shiva brushed her off, collapsed in an armchair, and put his smelly feet up on the seat next to her.

Parvati understood now that any of her husband's followers would never answer to her. So the next time she wanted to be alone, she also took matters into her own hands.

· · · · ·

IT WAS ANOTHER DULL AFTERNOON, calling Parvati to relax. Again, her husband was out, and she was happy to while away the afternoon by herself. But this time, she ensured she would not be disturbed.

She glanced at the golden root of turmeric she kept in her room and grasped it with all four of her palms. Its spicy fragrance hung in the air as she worked and fashioned it into the shape of a boy with four arms, just like hers. Then she gently opened her mouth and exhaled a magic breath onto it. The turmeric boy began to stretch and wiggle. And, just like that, Ganesh was born.

"You are my son," Goddess Parvati said, smiling at her lovely creation. "And I will love and revere you, just as you will me, your mother.

"Please go into the hallway and

guard the entry to the chambers. I want some time to myself without being disturbed, especially by Lord Shiva."

Ganesh bowed to show his mother respect and did as he was asked.

When Lord Shiva returned home that day and came upon the door to the chambers, he was irritated to see someone blocking his way. And it was a little boy, too—one he'd never seen before.

"What are you doing in my home, at the door to my chambers?" Shiva boomed with his powerful voice.

"I am protecting it for the goddess Parvati, who does not wish to be disturbed," Ganesh replied, with head and chest upright and proud.

"Boy, I order you to let me through!"

"You may not," Ganesh said.

"Who are you to tell me I cannot enter my own chambers!" Shiva said, his rage growing by the second.

Ganesh did not reply, but stood strong. Shiva tried to get around him, but it was as if the boy had created an impenetrable force around the doorway. Quick to anger, Shiva called for his army of demons, who appeared immediately.

"Destroy him!" Shiva demanded.

The demons attacked Ganesh, first trying to cut him with their weapons. Ganesh darted around, and they all missed. Then they tried to knock him over with their brute strength. Ganesh stuck his feet to the ground and remained untouched. The demons tried everything they could, but the boy was unharmed.

Shiva knew he was up against something powerful. So with his own divine strength, Shiva—Supreme Being, God of gods—chopped off the head of Ganesh.

The thud of Ganesh's head hitting the ground alerted Parvati. She leaped from her sofa and went into the hallway, only to find the gruesome aftermath of the fight between her husband and her son.

"What have you done?!" Parvati screamed at Shiva. "You have beheaded our son!" She collapsed next to the headless Ganesh and began to weep, pummeling the ground in anger. Ganesh was still able to wrap his four arms around his mother in a hug before they all fell limp to the ground.

"Our son? What do you mean, 'our son'?" Shiva replied, incredulous.

"His name was Ganesh, meaning Lord of the People. I created him with my own hands, to be my loyal companion and watch over me," she told him, brushing the tears from her face.

At once, Shiva felt a terrible sadness and regret. He promised Parvati he would bring Ganesh back to life, no matter what.

Calling Brahma, the Creator God, to his side, Shiva said, "My fellow deity, please help me—I have wronged my wife and destroyed my son, Ganesh. Go to the forest and collect the head of the first animal you encounter and bring it back here."

Brahma went out and came back with the head of the wisest and most revered of animals: the elephant. Shiva placed the elephant head atop Ganesh's body, and breathed life back into him. Ganesh began to move, patting his elephant head with his four hands. His new trunk trumpeted with dismay, as Ganesh was not too happy with his new head.

"I have done it! I've restored my son Ganesh back to life. Parvati!" he called out to his wife.

Parvati emerged from her bedroom where she had lain weeping, and gasped when she saw Ganesh, who stood there swinging his trunk from right to left, trying to get a handle on what was happening to him.

"No, no, no!" she pointed to Shiva in an accusing manner. "What is this? Am I supposed to be happy that our son now has an elephant's head?"

"But, my darling, I have brought Ganesh back to life! Our son is now as good as new," pleaded Shiva. "What else can I do to make this right?"

Parvati, exasperated with her bumbling husband, threw all her hands up in the air at once. There was a rush of wind as she did this, which nearly knocked Shiva over.

"You can make Ganesh the most preferred of all deities, forever worshipped first before all other gods," she said, and nodded her head once in finality. Ganesh nodded, too. He seemed to be happy with this decree.

Shiva promised Parvati he would see that Ganesh was worshipped first, and he devised a competition that would make this so. Shiva gathered all the gods at a starting line that he had drawn in gold. He and Parvati sat on a dais to oversee the competition.

"My fellow gods," he cried. "I challenge you to a race! The first god to traverse the great expanse of the universe and return to this line will be the winner. This god will be declared the most loved among the people and shall be worshipped first."

Each of the gods—Vishnu, Brahma, Krishna, and more—approached the starting line atop winged chariots, speedy horses, and bolts of lightning. Ganesh lumbered up to the starting line on the back of his trusty rat, Mooshika. Together, the pair were not fast, but they were clever.

"Ready, set, go!" shouted Shiva, and all the gods took off, leaving divine dust behind them. Ganesh and Mooshika inched forward.

But Shiva had known that while Ganesh was not first in speed, he was supreme in intelligence. Sure enough, Ganesh inched his way up to the dais where his parents were sitting and circled slowly around them. He then rode Mooshika back to the starting line, where Shiva declared him the winner!

When the other gods returned and found Ganesh to be the winner, they asked Shiva to explain why.

He told them, "Anyone who circles around his parents is one who crosses the whole universe."

And so the four-armed, elephant-headed god Ganesh became the foremost god over all others.

○— AND, EVEN TODAY, —○
THE LORD OF THE PEOPLE
IS STILL WIDELY LOVED
AND WORSHIPPED FIRST
BY THE HINDU PEOPLE.

Pangu
and
Nuwa

FROM CHINESE MYTHOLOGY

From the middle of the dark and vast universe swirling with stars and rocks, a giant black egg emerged. It glittered like the cosmos itself, twinkling with constellations but also roiling with disorder. Inside the egg, the conflicting forces of yin and yang mixed and tumbled, swirling together and apart by a raging wind. **YIN**: dark, lunar, cold, and feminine. **YANG**: light, solar, warm, and masculine.

In the middle of this black egg, a creature was born: Pangu, a giant covered in hair, with two horns on top of his head and two tusks protruding from his face. He remained curled in the fetal position, with a magical ax lying at his side. There Pangu lay and grew bigger over 18,000 years, with yin and yang becoming more ordered as time passed.

After thousands of years, Pangu awoke inside the egg. It was dark and silent as night. The nascent giant felt enclosed within something, but did not know what it was. So he began stretching his arms and legs until something cracked. It was the egg's shell! Pangu continued pushing the

CENTRAL
ASIA

WESTERN
ASIA

EASTERN
ASIA

SOUTHERN
ASIA

Sea of
Okhotsk

Sea
of
Japan

East China
Sea

PACIFIC
OCEAN

Arabian
Sea

Bay of
Bengal

South
China
Sea

Philippine
Sea

INDIAN
OCEAN

SOUTH-
EASTERN
ASIA

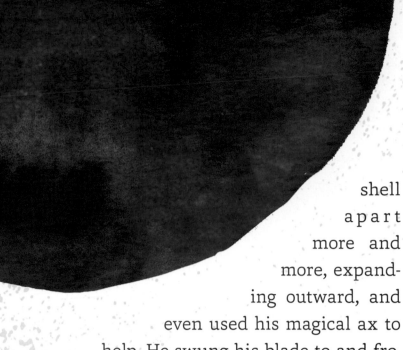

shell
a p a r t
more and
more, expand-
ing outward, and
even used his magical ax to
help. He swung his blade to and fro, splitting yin and yang apart. The darker half, yin, sank down and became the Earth. The lighter half, yang, became the sky. Pangu was pleased with this, as the Earth and sky felt as though they should be two separate things.

At this point, the Earth and sky were still very close together. Pangu was worried the two halves would collapse onto each other and seal up again, so he came between them and pushed them apart—his arms sending yang upwards and his feet sending yin downwards. With his efforts, the two halves moved away from each other over time: with each day, the sky rose 10 feet and the Earth lowered 10 feet. And each day, Pangu

grew 10 feet longer. For another 18,000 years, Pangu pushed upwards and downwards, growing and expanding the world to what we now know it to be. He was a dedicated soul.

When Pangu was absolutely certain that the Earth and sky were far enough apart that they would not fall onto one another, he considered his job done. Pangu had finally settled both yin and yang into their rightful places and secured them. And with the satisfaction of a job well done, Pangu collapsed. As he lay dying, his final breath morphed into rushing wind and dewy clouds. His voice boomed into thunder and the glint from his eyes became lightning. In his death, Pangu's left eye rose into the sky and became the sun, while his right eye circled the Earth as its moon. Then Pangu's body broke into parts—arms, legs, hands, feet, and torso—and became mountains and hills. The blood that had once coursed through his veins turned into rivers flowing between those hills. His flesh covered the Earth and became fertile land, budding with trees, grasses, and flowers. Pangu's sweat turned into rainwater and fell upon the fertile land. His bones sank into the ground to become prized jewels and mineral deposits; his teeth soon followed, and turned into precious metals underground. Pangu's hair, horns, and tusks whirled into outer space, becoming galaxies.

Pangu's death had given life to the Earth, but for thousands of years the world was a beautiful but lonely place, as there were no people to enjoy its bounty. That is, until the goddess Nuwa roamed the wild and dazzling Earth.

Nuwa was formed from the yin and yang that Pangu had once separated. Bits of sky and bits of earth had combined to form this strong goddess, and she felt right at home in her environment. But just like Pangu had been, Nuwa was alone in the world and eventually wanted some company.

At first, the sun and moon, wind and water were her happy companions, but one day she walked to the muddy banks of the Yellow River and saw her reflection. She realized there were none in the world who looked like her, or who could talk or think like her. She longed to laugh with friends, to share ideas with companions, to love someone.

Out of the mud from the Yellow River's banks, Nuwa began forming little figures, then animating them with her powers. She patted the first figure until it was fully molded, and placed it down on the ground. The tiny mud woman did a jig, so happy was she to be alive.

"Thank you, goddess Nuwa, for creating me!" the little woman said. Nuwa smiled and felt a happy satisfaction throughout her body. She set to work making more humans in this way. Little men and women of clay hopped out of her

hands and mingled with each other, each one thanking her for the privilege of being alive. With this, Nuwa began populating the Earth.

After creating the first hundred, she set to work making more, but her hands were getting very tired. Nuwa realized that it would take an eternity for her to make enough people to fill up the vast Earth. And so she grabbed a branch from a nearby tree, dragged it along the muddy banks, and flung drops of mud onto the land. As they hit the ground, they sprang little feet and began running this way and that, turning into thousands more little humans. With a few more

flicks of her wrist, Nuwa had populated the entire Earth!
However, she saw that as her humans died, there
would be the need to make more of them.
So clever Nuwa split the humans
into female and male.

**THIS WAY, THEY COULD
REPRODUCE THEMSELVES,
ALLOWING HER TO**
ENJOY AND ADMIRE WHAT SHE HAD
CREATED FOR ALL TIME.

Nyai Loro Kidul, Queen of the Sea

FROM INDONESIAN MYTHOLOGY

Nyai Loro Kidul—a fierce sea goddess and powerful mermaid with beauty intense enough to stir the currents, ruler of the violent Indian Ocean waves and shape-shifter extraordinaire—began her life as a girl on land.

Once upon a time, she was a princess named Dewi Kadita who lived during the reign of the Pajajaran kingdom, in West Java, Indonesia. Gifted with stunning beauty and a sharp mind, Dewi Kadita was one of the king's many offspring. During the time of the Pajajaran kingdom, it was customary for the king to have multiple wives and lots of children.

The wives and daughters lived separately from the king and his sons, in a luxurious palace that overlooked the aqua Indian Ocean. In the morning, the sunrise would pour through enormous east-facing windows and beckon them from their soft pillows. At night, they enjoyed colorful sunsets, lounging around on spacious verandas. They had all they could ever desire: the best food, expensive perfumes, fine clothing, and exquisite furniture. But some had more than others. . . .

Even though it was never said out loud, Dewi Kadita and her mother were favored by the king. Dewi Kadita's mother was intelligent, beautiful, and funny—and she passed all these wonderful traits on to her daughter. It was no secret that the king valued their company most, and he called on the pair more than any of his other wives and daughters. They were allowed to visit the king's

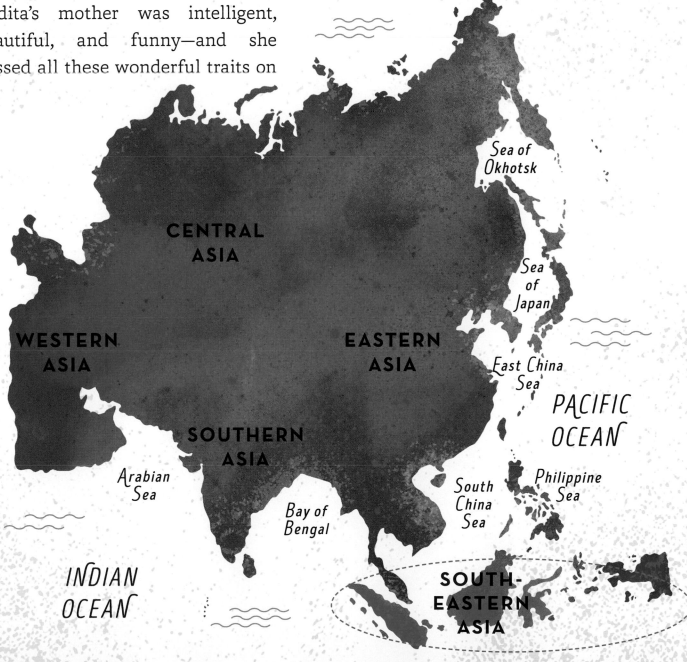

palace several times per year; the other women, only on festival days.

And perhaps it was true the king enjoyed their company the most. But the other wives and daughters were convinced the pair were also given more fine silks to wear, more expensive oils to condition their hair, and more powders to make their faces radiant. And once Dewi Kadita grew to be a young woman, rumors began to spread of the king's plan to arrange for her the highest marriage of all the daughters. The rest of the women were extremely jealous.

But Dewi Kadita and her mother did not notice this jealousy. They were pure of heart and assumed kindness in other people, just as they were kind themselves. Of course, this made the other wives and daughters even angrier. And when anger, hate,

and jealousy become lodged deep in one's heart, it produces a destructive venom within....

One afternoon when Dewi Kadita and her mother were visiting the king's palace, the other women hatched a plot against the princess.

"I know a witch . . . ," one of the mothers whispered slyly, afraid to speak loudly for there were guards everywhere. The other mothers nodded knowingly. Each pulled her daughter close in an embrace that reassured them all. "We will ruin Dewi Kadita soon enough."

The following week, Dewi Kadita and her mother sat down in their chambers to enjoy their tea. The princess took one sip and dropped her teacup on the ground, shattering it into a thousand pieces. She grabbed her burning throat.

"Mama, something is terribly wrong!" she shouted, and knocked the teacup out of her mother's hand. Her mother screamed as Dewi Kadita began to morph into something disgusting. Searing pain spread throughout the young woman's body. It started from her throat and quickly consumed her face, torso, arms and legs, and finally her hands and feet.

The princess could only see her hands, but they looked terrifying. Gnarled, scaly, and reddened skin replaced what had once been smooth and delicate. Aqua-green fingernails sprouted from the ends of each finger. It was as if her skin was turning inside out, and each moment of the transformation felt like a year's worth of agony. Finally, her whole body went numb.

Dewi Kadita looked to her mother for comfort. A moment's horror flashed upon the elder woman's face before she opened her arms to her daughter. The princess collapsed into her mother's arms and wept.

Later that day, Dewi Kadita summoned the courage to look in a mirror. She turned away in shock, but then looked at herself again. Her skin was scaly and hardened, and had turned a silvery gray. All of her hair had fallen out. The once-fair princess now looked like a revolting fish. When she saw what she had become, she knew she could never present herself in the kingdom again, for she would bring nothing but shame to her mother and father. She confessed this to her mother.

"MY DARLING GIRL,

I WILL NEVER BE ASHAMED OF YOU," HER MOTHER REPLIED.

access to black magic. She has done this to you and means us harm," her mother said. For as Dewi Kadita had been morphed by black magic, her mother too had morphed—through worry and fear. Where her body was once upright and lithe, it was now bent and broken. Even her clothes had begun to fray at the edges, just like her nerves. Her hair began to frazzle and frizz, and—although she was unaware of it at the time—stress had begun to unravel her mind. But the woman still had a spark in her, the same quality of light that shone within the princess.

⊶ SO DEWI KADITA AND HER ⊷ MOTHER COVERED THEMSELVES FROM HEAD TO TOE

AND FLED THE KINGDOM.

"Dewi Kadita, you are so much more than just your beauty. You have strength, you have humor, and you have a light within you that shines brighter than the sun reflecting off the sea.

"But we must flee the kingdom straightaway. Someone here has

There was no time to even bid goodbye to her father, the king. They hoped he would remember them the way they once were: happy and elegant.

They had no idea where to go, as they had never traveled before, but they wandered the countryside seeking help from strangers. The women were inherently good people, and this shone through their wizened and scaly appearances. Unfortunately, few people lived outside the kingdom, and so food and shelter for Dewi Kadita and her aging mother were scarce.

They wandered down into lush, green valleys, across the rims of active volcanoes, and sometimes took shelter in empty temples overnight. Constantly worried about their survival, the princess's mother grew worse. And as her health suffered, her mind did too—and her bouts of depression grew more severe. Dewi Kadita was still a strong young woman despite her new grotesque features. But as she watched her mother grow weaker, she began to lose faith.

Months went by. Her mother could barely walk now. She could barely even speak. Dewi Kadita found a damp cave for them to rest in one night. As the moon began its ascent in the sky, the young woman rubbed her mother's calloused feet and sang gently to her, trying to ignite her old spark. Her mother opened her eyes wide with love and tried to speak to her daughter, but could only muster a smile.

As she relaxed into her daughter's song, the old woman felt a peace that she thought had been lost. She suddenly had a vision of her daughter's future, full of strength and grace and reclaimed beauty. The moon was now high and bright, and pulled at the mother like a tide. She sat and lifted her head for a moment.

"I AM NOT LONG FOR THIS WORLD,"

she managed to say to Dewi Kadita. "Do not fear, for I have seen that you will rise to glory. Go to the water, my darling daughter."

"But, Mama . . . what do you mean? You must go on. *We* must go on together!" Dewi Kadita said with sadness and desperation in her heart.

"Go to the sea…," the mother whispered. And with that, she collapsed. The old woman closed her eyes for the last time.

Dewi Kadita picked up her dead mother and cradled her as if she were the parent. Her body bent like a tidal wave over her mother's body and tears rushed out. *How am I to go on without her?* Dewi Kadita thought. She felt weak, powerless. Her mother was her fierce protector, her support and strength, and her constant teacher. The princess realized she would now have to be all these things for herself.

And what of her mother's dying words? "Go to the water . . ." The pair had been traversing inland for so long, staying away from the shore, since that was the very place they had fled from—the coastline where the kingdom stretched, and where she vowed she would never show her horrible, scaly self. But her mother had always possessed knowledge that Dewi Kadita found mystifying, and she knew she had to seek out the sea.

It was nearing midnight now, when all would be closing their eyes to sleep. Dewi Kadita knew that this time of night might be safe to head toward the kingdom. She quickly buried her dear mother in a place where the moon could shine down on her grave. Then Dewi Kadita began her heavy trek toward the ocean.

Now standing upon the edge of a rocky outcropping, Dewi Kadita braced herself. The wind blew into her face as the violent waves crashed at her feet. What was she to do now? She was here at the water, her mother's dying wish. Now what?

As a giant wave swelled and surged up toward her, she flinched. But as the water slid down her battered legs, Dewi Kadita noticed it had removed the scaly flesh and left behind skin as smooth and radiant as a pearl.

DEWI KADITA COULD NOT BELIEVE HER EYES!

So this was what her mother had meant . . .

WITHOUT ANOTHER MOMENT'S THOUGHT, THE PRINCESS

LEAPED INTO THE WAVES,

which tossed and thrashed and pulled her under. As magically as her curse had first appeared, now it completely vanished. The water washed over her body, curing everything that had plagued her. Once again, Dewi Kadita was a beautiful, young woman full of humor and intellect. She laughed again, a big, hearty laugh. Where she had felt weak, both inside and out, she now had super strength. She flexed and twisted her muscular body. Her hair flowed with the currents. Her eyes shone with bioluminescence. Her skin was as radiant as ever. In place of her legs was now an iridescent tail that swished from side to side.

Dewi Kadita swam down into the depths, where the spirits of the sea were calling to her. When she reached the very bottom of the ocean, the sea spirits cheered.

"Our new Queen of the South Sea!"

they called as they bowed in respect.

"Your crowned name is Nyai Loro Kidul," one of the female spirits came forward to explain. "You now control the waves of the Indian Ocean. You alone are the most powerful one."

The new queen noticed that she was able to shape-shift and change herself from mermaid to whale, to shark, to old woman, to young woman, and back to mermaid—as quickly as she could think. She began twirling her body, noticing that a whirlpool began to form and suck up everything in its wake. Nyai Loro Kidul smiled.

"Now what you do with your power, my queen, is entirely up to you . . ." the spirit suggested.

As that morning's sunrise came upon the kingdom where Dewi Kadita and her mother had once lived,

IT WAS A TSUNAMI —NOT STREAMING LIGHT— THAT POURED INTO EACH AND EVERY EASTERN-FACING WINDOW.

MYTHS OF
...
OCEANIA

The Southern Hemisphere is abundant with colorful fauna, flora, and stories. In these stories, nature is revered and spirits reign supreme. Oral traditions are strong among Australian aboriginal and Polynesian people alike, which means that fascinating tales like these three have survived and delighted for generations.

The Legend of Māui

FROM POLYNESIAN MYTHOLOGY

Māui was half human and half god, and moved about the Pacific Ocean playing clever pranks and making trouble. He was a great trickster, but he almost never existed at all. . . .

Māui was the youngest of five brothers, but because he was born prematurely, his mother Taranga and father Makea-Tutara decided to fling him into the ocean. Sea spirits found little Māui, wrapped him in seaweed, and quickly delivered him to Tama-nui-te-rā, the sun god, who revived him and nurtured him into adulthood in the land of the gods.

Māui kept the gods and ancestors entertained with his endless tricks. As Māui grew, he became strong and powerful, like the immortals among whom he lived. And while he now possessed the magic of the gods, he had a human form so he could walk among mortals.

In fact, one day he walked right back to his mother's home and boldly reclaimed his rightful place among his brothers! The family accepted Māui back into the fold. But he was still the youngest and smallest, and his brothers thought he caused too much mischief. They often taunted him, calling him Māui-pōtiki, or "Māui the Last Born." Māui thought his brothers were brutes, so he ignored their insults.

Māui's brothers were all skilled fishermen and enjoyed nothing more than being out on the open water. Every day, his brothers would take their rods, lines, hooks, and canoe out on the ocean, and every day, Māui would ask to join. Māui's brothers always said no.

"And why not?" Māui would ask.

"You'll get us in trouble," they told him, referring to his trickster ways.

"Plus, you don't have any fishing gear and you're not borrowing ours!" Every day, they'd sail off the sandy, golden shore into the vast ocean . . . without their little brother. And every day, Māui vowed he'd get aboard that canoe one way or another.

Instead, Māui spent time with his grandmother, who loved his sense of humor and charm. Like her grandson, she also had a bit of magic in her. She enjoyed Māui's clever trickery, just like the gods who raised him. Māui's grandmother doted on him alone, since she thought the rest of her grandsons were rude.

ONE DAY, as Māui told her that he wanted to become a great fisherman, she popped out her jawbone and handed it to him. "Use this as a fishing hook, dear grandson, and great fortune will come to you at sea!" she told him.

"Thank you, Grandma Muri-ranga-whenua!" Māui said, hugging her.

"You're welcome, my little Māui.

One day, just when you need it, I will bestow upon you a great fish," his grandmother promised, pinching his cheek.

One night, while his brothers slept off another day full of salty sea air, Māui wove his own strong fishing line. Then he fashioned his grandmother's jawbone into a sharp hook. Perfect! He tied the hook to the line, then hid himself in his brothers' canoe.

Early the next morning, as the brothers pushed the canoe off the shore and into the ocean, they didn't notice sneaky Māui hiding in the hull. The strong brothers rowed and rowed until their canoe was very far away from land, and dropped anchor to begin fishing. When the boat was far away from shore, Māui knew he could reveal himself.

"Surprise!" Māui jumped out and shouted. His brothers stumbled over with shock.

"How did you get here?" they spat. The brothers were annoyed that Māui had tricked them into letting him on their fishing trip. But Māui told them that it was his destiny to be the greatest fisherman who ever lived, and he'd help them catch the biggest haul of fish they'd ever seen.

"How are you going to do that, little Māui-pōtiki?" his biggest brother scoffed.

Māui puffed out his chest and began chanting a karakia, or prayer, to the sea god:

KUKU, KUKU IKA,
KUKU WEHIWEHI,
TĀKINA KO KOE NĀ,
TE IHO O IKA,
TE IHO O TĀNGAROA—
UARA KI UTA RĀ,
UARA KI TAI RĀ.

As Māui's chant skimmed along the water and echoed deep into the sea, the brothers dropped their hooks. They caught the biggest haul of fish they had ever seen! Snappers, groupers, pufferfish, and eels. Yellowfins, halibut—they even caught some deep-sea squid. Soon their canoe was heaving with fish.

"Well done, little Māui! We've caught more today than we have in our whole lives," they exclaimed, with eyes dazzling and mouths watering.

Now it was Māui's turn, but when he took out his fishing line, the brothers burst into laughter.

"Look at that odd-shaped hook!" They sneered at the hook Māui had fashioned from his grandmother's jawbone. "Even with your powerful karakia, that thing won't even be able to snare the smallest fish."

Māui paid them no attention. "My hook may be strange, but it's still more powerful than yours," he said. At that, the brothers doubled over again with hysterical laughter. Māui turned red and hot, and clenched his fist tight around the hook, drawing blood. He left the blood on the hook for bait, and—glaring at his brothers—tossed his line into the water. The whole time, he continued to chant his karakia.

Māui only had to wait a few moments before his line went taut. He had caught something! Whatever had bitten Māui's hook was still moving—and fast. It dragged the small canoe by Māui's fishing line, right across the water. Faster and faster and faster the vessel went, with each burly brother grabbing hold of the sides for dear life.

"Cut the line! Cut the line!" they shouted to Māui. "It's going to pull us under!" The brothers were afraid, but Māui was not.

He pulled that gigantic fish right up to the surface—and who was laughing now? The fish was massive, much bigger than the canoe, and stretched as far as they could see in both directions. It was so smooth that the sun reflected off its back.

"This is the sacred fish that Muri-ranga-whenua, our grandmother, promised she would bestow upon me," Māui said. "It's finally come! I am going to invite our family to help us enjoy this bounty. You must guard this behemoth while I'm gone."

The brothers agreed to guard the fish with their lives, and Māui swam back to shore to call upon their elders. Māui returned with the elders, and as they approached they could see the fish even from a great distance. The elders were so amazed to see the giant fish, they declared, "All

hail Māui—the best fisherman who ever lived!" They cheered and celebrated, knowing their family would remain in good fortune now that they had this enormous fish.

But as they got closer, they saw that the greedy brothers had chopped up the fish for themselves, each arguing over who was to get which piece. They had mangled the beautiful, smooth fish that Māui had caught, and caused its flesh to form mountains and valleys.

Māui was angry—but not too shocked—at his brothers' greed. How could he have trusted these scoundrels with his grandmother's sacred fish?

"Brothers, you will pay for this!" he shouted at them, as he glared and shook his hook in their direction.

And indeed, they did: when the elders saw what they had done, they rejected the selfish brothers in favor of the great Māui.

Māui's glorious fish became the North Island of New Zealand, with tall mountains and deep valleys, and plants, birds, and people.

AND MĀUI IS STILL FAVORED OVER HIS BROTHERS TO THIS DAY.

Uluru

This is the story of a rock. *A rock?* you might ask skeptically, with an open mouth suppressing a yawn. Ah, but this is no ordinary rock. This is Uluru.

Back in the beginning of time, when the face of the Earth was still being formed, the ancestors of the Anangu people appeared on the landmass that is known today as Australia. The Anangu are a group of aboriginal people who live primarily in the Central Western Desert. When their ancestors roamed a long time ago, the desert was wide and flat. That is, until Uluru—a colossal red sandstone rock—emerged and rose from the earth, as if by magic.

Uluru was instantly sacred to the Anangu, bearing great cultural and spiritual importance then, and now. The Anangu Dreamtime—or collection of origin stories—tells the tale of how each feature formed on that undulating, craggy rock. Each characteristic of the rock's face was created by a spirit. Each hole, rivulet, track, and spine of the monolithic rock Uluru has its own story.

During the creation of the Earth, two tribes of snake people came to be. One group was devoted to the nonvenomous Kuniya, or the woma python. They lived in the east of Pugabuga—where a small body of water sat in the middle of the dry plains. The other group was the vicious Liru, dedicated to the poisonous snake, who lived west of Pugabuga. The Kuniya were gentle and water-seeking, while the Liru were dangerous, stalking through the rough desert lands. Since unforgiving terrain separated the two groups, however, they did not clash often.

Over time, Pugabuga was not enough for the Kuniya. They left and traveled west until they arrived at a huge sand hill that was smooth and flat on top. There was a bountiful water hole on the plateau, and the Kuniya decided to set up camp and make this spot their new home.

This turned out to be a blessed choice. For a time, life was very good for the Kuniya. There was wildlife to hunt, like kangaroos, wallabies, and emus. Sweet fruits, hearty yams, and crunchy seeds blossomed around the water source. The Kuniya thrived and raised their families in peace, each family in its own happy camp.

The magic surrounding the land was strong, bonding the Kuniya to that sacred place.

Timor Sea

Arafura Sea

AUSTRALIA

Great Australian Bight

Solomon Sea

Coral Sea

Tasman Sea

PACIFIC OCEAN

The Kuniya carved homes into the side of the sand hill which, over time, hardened and became spacious caves. They also formed deep ridges in the sides of the rock by trekking to and from the water hole daily. Even the elder Kuniya men made grooves in the rock as their long beards dragged along the ground. And when the Kuniya passed on to the afterlife, their bodies became part of the rock formation.

Over many years, the land transformed into the giant rock called Uluṟu. Life was happy for the Kuniya . . . until the Liru found them. The venomous group was living in the enormous mountain called Kata Tjuṯa, but when the Liru saw the Kuniya living in prosperity on Uluṟu, they became jealous.

So the Liru planned an attack on the Kuniya. The young Liru warriors crept up to Uluṟu from the southwest. Led by a warrior named Kulikudgeri, they carried clubs, knives, and spears to make their power known.

The first camp the Liru approached was that of a powerful Kuniya woman named Bulari, who had recently given birth and set up a separate camp to nurture and bond with her newborn. Bulari was fiercely protective of her child. She spied the Liru sneaking up to the Kuniya camp, and without a

moment to spare, she sprang to her feet and clutched her baby tightly. She charged toward the Liru warriors while spitting out *arukwita*, the spirit of disease and death. She was not afraid of any man who threatened her or her people.

The *arukwita* spiraled as it sprang from Bulari's mouth, twisting the Liru warrior's body. Many of the men were killed, but the survivors lurched toward Bulari, shouting threats and curses upon her. Since there were many Liru, Bulari and her baby did not stand a chance. As the Liru closed in and killed Bulari and her newborn, the victims' spirits melded with the sacred rock. Bulari turned into a shallow cave on the side of Uluṟu. Her baby became a set of small, uneven rocks at its edge.

The Liru continuing their raid soon found the entire Kuniya camp and attacked with full force. The Kuniya were harmless: no match for the vicious Liru.

BUT STILL, THEY WERE BRAVE.

A young Kuniya warrior came forward to challenge Kulikudgeri to a fight to the death. The Kuniya warrior wanted to stop the attack on his people once and for all, so he charged at Kulikudgeri and slashed him. Although badly injured, Kulikudgeri fought back hard, slashing the young Kuniya warrior with every assault. At the end of the terrible battle, Kulikudgeri dealt a fatal stab to his opponent. Profusely bleeding, the young man dragged himself over the sand hill, where he died. The stumbling track he left became a stream. Today, there are three water holes filled with water that was once his blood.

The mother of the slain warrior, Kuniya Inkridi, witnessed the whole bloody battle and charged at Kulikudgeri with fury, hoping to kill the one who had murdered her son. The woman struck his nose with a giant stick, cutting it off and mortally wounding the great Liru warrior. Kulikudgeri died in anguish, blood streaming down his body and over the surface of the land. After his death, his body became a large, square boulder, stained red. His severed nose now lies near the boulder as a huge slab of stone split from its body.

MEANWHILE, THE BATTLE CONTINUED BETWEEN THE LIRU AND KUNIYA.

It was vicious. It was bloody. It was over quickly. The Liru, with their plentiful clubs, knives, and spears, easily conquered the Kuniya. Although they fought as hard as they could, the Kuniya could not defeat the Liru in the surprise attack and most of them perished in the battle.

Liru spears made pockmarks on one side of Uluṟu where soldiers had attacked. Desert oaks—which are said to be the bodies of the Liru warriors—line the path where they snuck up on the Kuniya. The path of plunder turned into deep cracks on the southwestern side of the rock. The events of this epic battle and the bodies of those who perished were preserved within the rock of Uluṟu. The giant sand hill had fully and finally solidified.

THEIR STORY OF
BLOOD AND TEARS
MADE ULU<u>R</u>U WHAT IT IS TODAY.

The Rainbow Serpent

FROM THE ABORIGINAL PEOPLE
OF AUSTRALIA

In the time before any-thing existed, the Earth was just a sphere of rock: cold and dark, smooth and completely dry. Nothing lived yet. No plants grew. No creatures crept. No water flowed.

Beneath the surface, the Rainbow Serpent lay sleeping. She was breathtakingly beautiful, her scaly back a true rainbow of iridescent colors. The Rainbow Serpent also had the power to create. But she lay hidden underneath the cold, dark ground.

Inside her belly slept every animal that would ever be—all dormant and waiting to be born.

One day, the Rainbow Serpent woke and crawled up to the surface of this unforgiving Earth. She stretched her long body this way and that, her stiff muscles uncoiling and lengthening.

"What could this place be?" she wondered. For really, there was not much to be seen on the landscape—if you could even call it a landscape. But the terrain from where she had just emerged now formed a lovely slope—a small mountain. She noticed that in the place where she had stretched her long body to wake it up, there was now a smooth track. The Rainbow Serpent realized the malleable earth bent to her form, so she began traveling all over the land, winding back and forth, making deep indentations in the ground.

As the serpent slithered and stirred, the large, hot sun rushed out from her mouth and brightened the sky. Then the iridescent colors of her rainbow body leaped up in an arc to join the sun. How joyful this new Earth was becoming! The Rainbow Serpent began to sing as she traveled, making great gorges, valleys, ridges, and mountains with her body.

As she sang, all the animals lying dormant in her belly suddenly woke up. The land and sky animals emerged, slowly and carefully, into the light. Mammals, reptiles, birds, and insects of all kinds walked right out of the Rainbow Serpent's open mouth and onto the newly forming Earth.

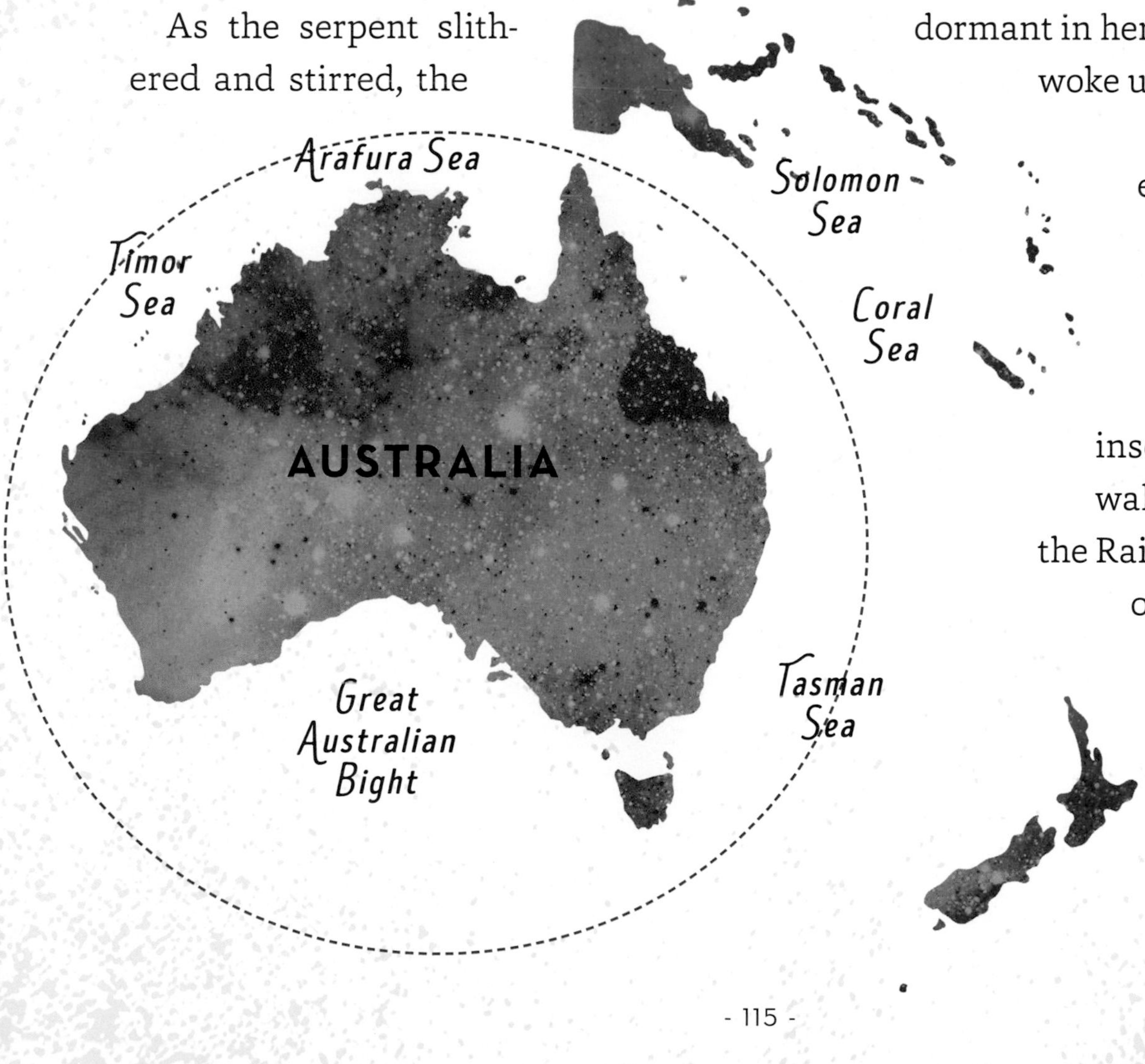

Arafura Sea

Timor Sea

Solomon Sea

Coral Sea

AUSTRALIA

Great Australian Bight

Tasman Sea

"Welcome!" she greeted each one as it emerged. Then a funny, new kind of animal hopped out. A frog. Hundreds of them—no, thousands—leaped from the Rainbow Serpent's mouth. The frogs were giant and heavy, hopping out sluggishly, looking uncomfortably full of something. Once they were all out in the world, the Rainbow Serpent tickled their bellies. The frogs opened their mouths wide to laugh, and out poured floods of water that filled up the deep tracks made by the Rainbow Serpent all over the land. This is how the oceans, rivers, lakes, and streams all came to be.

And so it was that grass and trees were now able to grow lush and tall. The new animals of the Earth were able to drink and thrive. The other amphibians and fish sleeping in the Rainbow Serpent's belly could come out and join the bustling scene. As it is now on Earth, each creature found its place in the world, some on the land, some in the water, and some in the sky.

The animals of the Earth revered the Rainbow Serpent for creating the land and bringing them sacred water, which they knew to be a precious thing. Since the Rainbow Serpent had made the elements, she also made the laws for each place, essentially ruling over the world. Anyone who dared to break these laws and disrespect nature would be turned to stone and fused into the landscape, rather than be able to enjoy the beautiful Earth. So each living creature honored the beautiful Rainbow Serpent by working hard to care for the land and water. But of course, there were a small few who lacked respect.

Some of the animals began to fight over food, which was strictly against the law. The Rainbow Serpent immediately turned them to stone. A cheetah became a boulder, and a lion became an island. A small group of ants was turned into pebbles. She turned two vicious seagulls into peninsulas. Two sharks fighting over the same fish suddenly transformed

into coral and dropped down to the seafloor. So many creatures broke the Rainbow Serpent's laws that the landscape became even more varied and interesting.

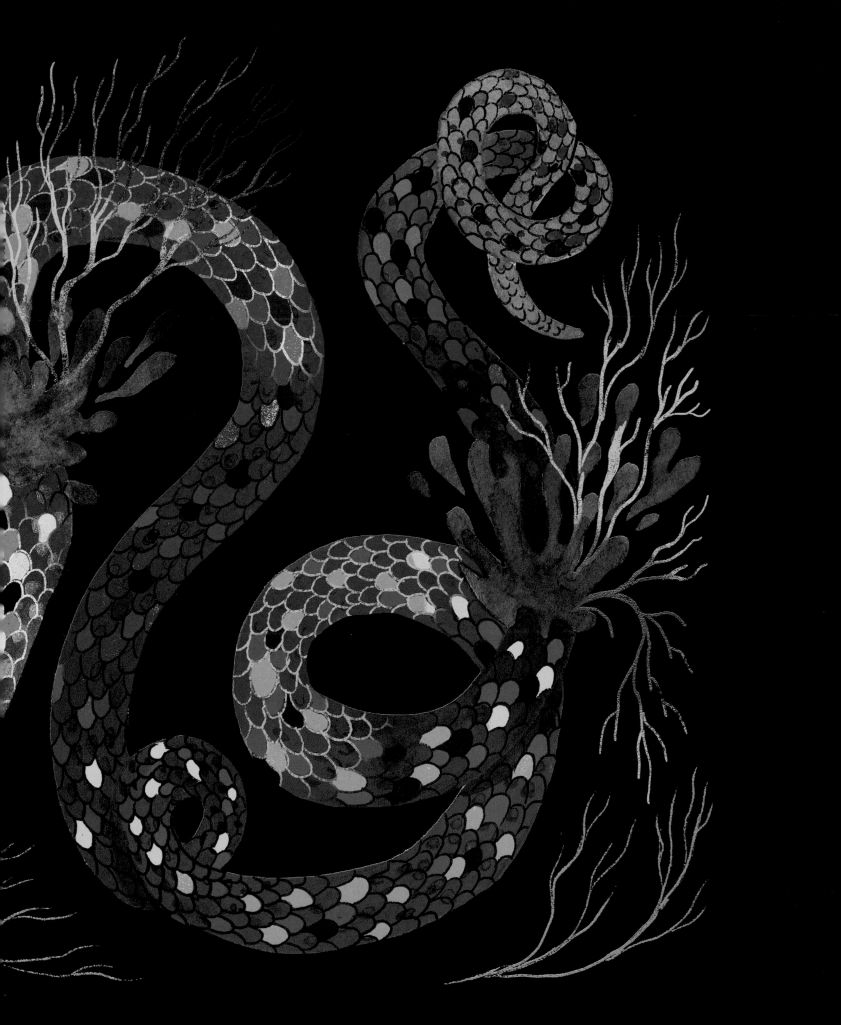

But the animals who did obey the law were happy and healthy. The Rainbow Serpent saw to that. She turned some of the especially well-behaved ones into humans, each with a talisman signifying their original form—whether mammal, reptile, amphibian, fish, bird, or insect. These new humans were given tools to work the land, and families to enjoy their days with.

The descendants of these first humans say that when a rainbow appears in the sky, it is the Rainbow Serpent curving her back across the beautiful land she created. They still consider the land and water sacred; they honor the Rainbow Serpent as their ancestors did and recount stories about her.

Now that the Earth had been formed and populated with animals and early humans, the Rainbow Serpent commenced a long slumber. For many years, she lay dormant. When she finally woke again, she emerged as Goorialla and took a male form.

Goorialla felt lonely.

"I need to find my people," he said to no one, for no one was around. Fortunately, Goorialla could move fast and efficiently across the land, without wasting much time. He moved quickly from the south of Australia to the north, making ravines and mountains with his long, powerful body.

Suddenly, faint voices carried by the wind made it to Goorialla's keen ears. But the voices were not speaking a language he understood, and he decided that they could not be from his people. He moved on, creating many more tracks on his journey. Several more times, Goorialla thought he heard distant voices. But these, too, were not in a language he understood.

After about a week of travel, Goorialla heard joyful, singing voices. At last, he understood the words they were singing!

"Finally, I have found my people!" Goorialla exclaimed and followed the sound of the voices until the singing got louder. When he arrived at the camp, he saw that his people

were having a raucous party. That's why they were singing. They were also dancing a serpent-like dance, and Goorialla danced with them, falling in line as if he had been there with his people all along. His hands fit perfectly into theirs, and his

voice melded with the others' in perfect harmony. Goorialla certainly had found his people, and he was overjoyed.

He was also tired from his long journey and the boisterous party. A storm was fast approaching, so Goorialla and his people built tents for shelter. They finished just as the rain came pouring down and the thunder crashed.

But not everyone had built a shelter. Two boys of the tribe, the Bil-bil brothers, needed a place to stay the night, and they ran to Goorialla's tent.

"May we please stay with you?" they implored.

"I have no room in my small tent," Goorialla told the brothers.

"But you may sleep in my mouth where it is warm and safe." He opened his mouth and the boys hesitated. But they walked inside, desperately needing a place to stay the night. As soon as Goorialla closed his mouth, he swallowed the boys. Gulp!

Oh no! What had Goorialla done? He immediately felt remorseful. It had been an accident! Now he was scared and worried about what his people would think when they found out he had swallowed the boys. For surely when they woke up and took stock of the tribe, they would know the boys were gone and would conduct a thorough search. So Goorialla left the camp in the middle of the night.

When the adults woke the next morning, of course they were angry. They immediately noticed the missing boys and went searching for Goorialla. It was surely his fault! Why else would he have left in the middle of the night? Fortunately for them, Goorialla had not gone too far, still tired and full from the night before.

The tribe found Goorialla asleep in the sun at the top of a small mountain, and they cut him open. The two boys emerged from Goorialla's open belly as beautiful rainbow lorikeets—they had been transformed into the colorful birds overnight—and they flew far away.

When Goorialla saw his belly had been split open by his own people, he was furious. How could they do this terrible thing to him? He thrashed and crashed in his fury, breaking up whole mountains, throwing rocks down at the people, and turning some of them into animals and trees.

Weary and angry, Goorialla then vanished into the sea forever, and the people and animals never saw him again. They were no longer worthy of Goorialla's presence on Earth,

BUT SOMETIMES—
WHEN THEY WERE VERY LUCKY—
THEY WERE ABLE TO GLIMPSE HIM
AS A RAINBOW
— IN THE SKY. —

MYTHS OF ...
THE AMERICAS

North, Central, and South America are attached by both land and strong oral traditions. There is a history of animism—in which a human-like soul is given to animals and objects—among native tribes of the Americas, which we see in these stories. Animals talk, spirits are conjured, and nature possesses the ultimate power.

Coyote Steals Fire for the People

FROM THE NATIVE AMERICAN PEOPLE
OF THE UNITED STATES

When the world was still brand-new, the Earth began turning with the seasons. The people were happiest when spring blossomed and ripened the trees; when summer dropped plump and delicious fruits into their arms; and when autumn cast deep, warm colors into their dreams. But the colors of autumn always faded, and then the pinpricks of frost came over the land, signaling winter.

For the people, winter was brutal. Each time the season rolled around, they became fearful and troubled, and some of the children and elders— the weaker ones of the tribe—died during the long, freezing nights. The people had heard of fire, this mythical warmth-giving thing, but they had never seen it before and did not know where it came from.

"If only we had fire to stay warm during the winter!" they moaned, huddling together and mourning the recent death of one of their infants.

Coyote, who with his thick coat had no need for fire, saw the people struggling year after year. Their wails made the fur on his back stand on end.

THEIR SADNESS CHILLED COYOTE TO HIS BONES.

In early spring, before the chill had fully loosened its grip, Coyote found his animal friends. He wanted to talk to them about helping the people.

"It seems the people are not able to cope with our harsh winters," Coyote said to Squirrel, Chipmunk, and Frog. "But we animals are able to survive the winter on our own."

Chipmunk nodded in agreement. "I hibernate..."

"So do I," Frog chimed in. "I sleep for months on a bed of mud beneath the frozen surface of the pond."

"And I spend winters in my den, which is warm enough for me," added Squirrel. "And you have nice warm fur," he said to Coyote.

"You're right, I am lucky," said Coyote. "The people are not so lucky. I think I know a way to help them. There is a mountaintop where the Fire-Beings live. I stumbled upon these mystical creatures one evening while

stalking the deep, enchanted parts of the forest. Do you know of them?" His friends all shook their heads.

"Well, these creatures are selfish and keep all the fire in the world to themselves, even though the people so desperately need it. They closely guard their fire night and day, afraid that giving away their precious gift might lessen their power. But I've heard there is one moment in the early morning when they let their guard down. In that moment, I will steal the fire for the people!"

Coyote told his friends that he needed their help, and they agreed to his plan.

Coyote, Squirrel, Chipmunk, and Frog set out for the camp of the Fire-Beings. The trail was still icy and just beginning to thaw, but the animals used their claws as they climbed the mountain where the Fire-Beings lived.

When they arrived close to the top of the mountain, it was the dead of night. From a distance, the animals could see the orange glow of the fire and smell the piquant smoke.

However, only Coyote was to approach the camp of the Fire-Beings so he could secretly grab the fire and run when the time came. The other animals stayed back, but not too far away, ready to help if necessary.

As Coyote crept closer, he made sure to keep quiet, slipping between the trees. He saw four Beings, each sitting on their own blackened tree stump, forming a circle around a crackling bonfire. Their bodies glowed red like coals and their eyes glinted like flint. At the ends of their fingers were long, vulture-like claws. Their fire reached as high as the tops of the ancient trees surrounding the clearing, and roared as it blazed.

"So this is fire . . . ," Coyote whispered to himself in awe.

"Who goes there?" screeched one of the Fire-Beings as they all rose to their feet.

"What do you want with us?" screeched another.

"It's nothing," said a third Being, peering directly at Coyote in his paltry hiding place. "Just a mangy coyote who has no need for fire." And the Fire-Beings turned away from him.

Coyote heaved a deep sigh and lay down on the ground, a few feet closer to the Fire-Beings' camp. They had mistaken him for an ordinary coyote and didn't care that he was there. *Well then,* Coyote thought. *All the easier to inch even nearer to the prize.*

With fallen pine needles, dried hickory scraps, and other detritus from the forest, the Fire-Beings fed their fire to grow to massive proportions. As the night wore on, each Fire-Being retreated to their shelter to sleep, one by one, until there was only one left on guard.

As the deep night lightened into dawn, the last Fire-Being yawned deeply. It was nearly his turn to sleep, and Coyote could tell he was getting weary. The Fire-Being slunk over to the shelter and called out, "Sister, come out here and watch the fire. I'm tired now and I want to rest."

"I'm coming," she replied, bleary-eyed and sluggish. But she did not come right away.

THIS WAS THE MOMENT FOR COYOTE TO MAKE HIS MOVE!

Seizing his chance, Coyote pounced—snatching a burning stick from the fire. He placed it carefully between his teeth and sprang away down the mountain with the stolen prize.

The Fire-Beings saw that they had been tricked. Shrieking, they flew down the mountain after him. As fast as Coyote could run, the Fire-Beings were faster. One of them reached out and grabbed the tip of Coyote's tail, singeing it white with fierce heat. This is why coyotes' tail tips are still white to this day.

Coyote yelped in pain and his friends immediately came to help.

"Squirrel, grab the fire!" Coyote shouted. He tossed the burning branch to Squirrel, who placed it on her back and ran. But the fire was too hot for Squirrel and it curled her tail right up and back, which is how squirrels' tails became this shape.

The Fire-Beings were too fast for

Squirrel, too, and they soon caught up with her.

"Chipmunk, take the fire!" Squirrel yelled to her friend, who caught the fire. But the Fire-Beings were catching up to him fast. As Chipmunk turned to run away, one of the Beings scratched down the length of his back with its steely claws, creating the three lines that you can still see on a chipmunk's back today.

Thankfully, Frog hopped alongside and grabbed the fire from Chipmunk's tiny claws. The Fire-Beings grabbed Frog's tail, trying to stop her. Frog wriggled free, still holding on to the fire, but left her tail behind, which is why frogs now don't have tails.

"Over here," yelled Wood, a gnarled tree trunk with two knots for eyes and a hollow opening for a mouth. "Toss the fire to me!"

Frog hopped as fast as possible toward Wood, just as the Fire-Beings were closing in.

She tossed the fire into Wood's mouth, which then closed. Everyone heard a faint sizzle as Wood swallowed the fire, and the chase ceased at once. The animals heaved with relief.

The Fire-Beings stopped in their tracks. They gathered together, blinking their flinty eyes and glowing redder with every second, but they did not know how to get the fire out of Wood. First, they tried to bribe it with gifts of smoke and light. But what use were these to Wood? Next, they sang enchanted songs, trying to coax the fire out of Wood. But Wood did not hear their songs. Becoming enraged, the Fire-Beings started to shout and threaten Wood with knives. But Wood was immune to these threats, and the Fire-Beings had to give up. Angry and defeated, the Fire-Beings trudged back to their mountaintop, knowing that a piece of their precious fire had been relinquished.

But Wood whispered to clever Coyote how to get the fire out of him! Coyote then went back to the people and showed them how to rub two dry wooden sticks together and spin a sharpened stick in a hole in another piece of wood.

"This is how you make heat . . . ," he told the people. "And eventually fire."

THE PEOPLE WOULD NEVER AGAIN SUFFER DURING FREEZING WINTERS. THEY WERE FOREVER GRATEFUL TO COYOTE FOR THE GIFT OF FIRE.

The White Buffalo Calf Woman

FROM THE LAKOTA PEOPLE
OF THE UNITED STATES

In the days before the Lakota had horses to aid them in hunting buffalo, a great famine befell the people. Food was scarce, and people ate mostly what they could forage, like nuts, berries, and seeds. But this was not enough, and their situation became dire; the very young and very old began to die of starvation. The Lakota chief sent out two warriors to hunt for food.

The warriors had great difficulty finding anything substantial to bring back to their people, so they climbed a mountain to get a better look at the land spread before them. In the distance, they spotted something mysterious. It was a figure, and it seemed to be floating, the tall grass parting as it glided across the plains. Was it an animal? It looked like a white buffalo, the rarest and most sacred of all creatures.

When the figure came closer, the warriors had a better view. It was a woman! She was very beautiful and young, with dark hair and skin and sparkling eyes the color of mahogany.

Dressed all in white buckskin, she shone with a supernatural brilliance.

"That is the White Buffalo Calf Woman," one of the warriors whispered. He couldn't believe he was in her holy presence, and it left him nearly breathless. "Perhaps she is an omen of good things to come?"

But the other warrior saw her through eyes of desire, and his only thought was to take her as his wife. "I want her," he said. He began to approach her, arms outstretched.

"What are you doing, my friend?" the other warrior tried to warn. "You cannot go near her, let alone touch her!" They both knew she was a supernatural being, and any sacrilegious behavior would be dangerous.

But the amorous warrior kept approaching the White Buffalo Calf Woman and embraced her in a way that was between hug and grasp. The White Buffalo Calf Woman did not move a muscle.

Then suddenly both figures were enveloped in a cloud of white smoke. An absolute silence followed. When the smoke cleared and the sounds of nature returned, the only

ARCTIC OCEAN

Bering Sea

Hudson Bay

NORTH AMERICA

PACIFIC OCEAN

ATLANTIC OCEAN

CARIBBEAN

Gulf of Mexico

CENTRAL AMERICA

Caribbean Sea

things left were the
mysterious woman and
the burned bones of the warrior. The White Buffalo Calf Woman
looked like she had not been touched at all.
  The bones were carelessly stacked in a heap.
    The second warrior was terrified. Would he,
    too, be turned into a pile of charred bones?
    He turned to run away but was stopped
    in his tracks. The White Buffalo Calf
      Woman addressed the man in his
        native tongue.
          "You are a good and
          respectful man," she

began. "Your heart and mind are pure. No harm will come to you." The White Buffalo Calf Woman beckoned him forward and he approached her with reverence and caution.

"You noticed correctly that I am a holy woman. Well done. The Lakota are in trouble, aren't they?" The man nodded. "Do as I say, and your people will rise again." Then she gave him instructions to return to his people, assemble the council, and explain to the chief how to prepare for her arrival.

The warrior did as he was told and returned to his people.

"I've seen the White Buffalo Calf Woman," he recounted. "She is as powerful as she is beautiful and has told me that our people will rise again. We must prepare for her arrival in four days by building a brand-new lodge big enough for all of us, held up by twenty-four poles and blessed for her. Then she will come and help us restore our prosperity."

The Lakota built a lodge large enough to fit the entire tribe and waited for her to come.

ON THEIR

FOURTH DAY OF WAITING,

············

the ground was shrouded in mist and there was a faint whistle on the breeze. The Lakota chief spotted something far off in the distance. The figure plodded slowly toward their camp. It was a white buffalo calf.

From this, the chief knew that she was the true White Buffalo Calf Woman who had the power to change form. As the buffalo calf approached the lodge where the whole tribe was waiting, her impressive white fur morphed into a gleaming buckskin cloak, beautifully embroidered. The calf's impenetrable eyes turned into mysterious dark human eyes. And the dark-rimmed ears of the calf shifted and grew into a flowing mane of silky black hair. Then the White Buffalo Calf Woman appeared before them, carrying a bundle.

"Welcome, sister. We are glad you have come to teach us," the chief addressed her. "We wish we had food to offer you, but we have fallen on hard times and only have water to give." He held out a bowlful of clear mountain water and showed her into the lodge, where the whole tribe was waiting.

As if there were no time to waste, the White Buffalo Calf Woman walked to the middle of the twenty-four poles used to construct the lodge. She placed her bundle down and began to instruct the Lakota people.

"You must build an *owanka wakan*, a sacred altar, in this very spot. Construct it using the plentiful red earth that surrounds you, then place a buffalo skull atop this altar," she commanded. The people did as they were told, building the altar, then placing a buffalo skull on top.

The White Buffalo Calf Woman approached the quickly built altar, closed her eyes, and smoothed her flat palm over the front of it. A small fire suddenly ignited.

It blazed, quiet and compact. "This is the *peta-owihankeshni*, the fire that will never end," she told them. "You will pass this fire down through generations of Lakota."

The White Buffalo Calf Woman reached into her bundle and took out the *chanunpa*, a sacred ceremonial pipe, holding it out in her two ethereal hands. The pipe was long and thin, with a small bowl on one end to hold tobacco. The blond-wood stem was carved and hollowed out with great care, while the bowl was made of dark stone with engravings that looked like the face of a buffalo. Several delicate feathers hung from a lanyard at the bowl's end.

The people took a good look at the beautiful and holy pipe, and how the White Buffalo Calf Woman was holding it—her right hand gripping the stem and the left hand cupping the bowl. "This is the only way to hold such a sacred pipe," she instructed, then began packing the bowl with deep-red tobacco.

Then as if taken by the spirit of Anpetu-Wi, the great sun, the White Buffalo Calf Woman methodically walked around the periphery of the lodge four times, four being the holiest number. "This loop represents the endless circle of life," she said as she came back to the altar.

She lit the pipe on the altar's never-ending fire, and as the smoke rose toward the heavens she told them, "This is the living breath of the Grandfather of Mystery, Tunkashila."

Then the White Buffalo Calf Woman began to chant hypnotizing melodies and stomp her feet rhythmically. She lifted the pipe up to the sky, down toward the Earth, then to the north, south, east, and west—consecrating both natural and spiritual worlds, the pipe binding all living things together. The people of the tribe followed along, chanting louder as they stomped their feet and moved their arms, with their left and right hands held outward as if each were grasping the sacred pipe. In this way, the White Buffalo Calf Woman taught the people the right way to pray, making the words and movements become part of their souls. She taught them how to reconnect with the land, which they so desperately needed.

"Come closer to the pipe," she said as she walked among the audience. "Do you see how it has seven rings carved into it? These represent the seven sacred ceremonies, which are to be the backbone of your spiritual lives." She then discussed these seven sacred ceremonies with the tribe, and how and when to perform them: THE SWEAT LODGE, a purification ceremony; THE NAMING CEREMONY, for newborn children; THE HEALING CEREMONY; THE MAKING OF RELATIVES, or peace-bringing ceremony; THE MARRIAGE CEREMONY; THE VISION QUEST, for finding one's spiritual guide; and THE SUN DANCE CEREMONY.

"Performed properly and at the correct times, these sacred ceremonies will bring you a heightened awareness of life and the world around you."

Then the White Buffalo Calf Woman addressed the women and children. "Women, I praise you! Do not think that just because your hands do not bring home the fruit that feeds your people that your work is less important than the men's. The work of your hands and the fruit of your bodies is just as sacred, if not more so. And children, you are even more important than your elders, as you are the future of the tribe. One day, you too will pray with the pipe and bring honor and prosperity to yourselves."

She turned to the Lakota chief. "My work here is done. I have taught you all you need to know, and you now have the sacred pipe. Use it well and use it properly, and you should have renewed abundance, as you wish.

"I shall come back to you one day to purify the world and bring harmony to all. The birth of a white buffalo will be a sign of my return," she finished, and shut her mouth in a firm line.

"Thank you, Sister, for what you have shown us. We will use the pipe and pray accordingly," the Lakota chief said as the White Buffalo Calf Woman turned and began to walk off in the direction from which she had come.

The people—some amazed by what they had experienced, some shocked—watched the White Buffalo Calf Woman grow smaller as she approached the sun setting on the horizon. With the blood-red orb sinking behind her, the White Buffalo Calf Woman stopped and rolled over four times. With the first roll, she turned into a black buffalo, next a brown buffalo, then a red buffalo, and—finally—a white buffalo, the most sacred living being. The people then knew they had witnessed something extraordinary that day. They vowed to keep their promises to the White Buffalo Calf Woman.

With the White Buffalo Calf Woman's departure, prosperity arrived. The herds of buffalo suddenly returned to their land, providing the people with the food and skins they needed to survive.

THE LAKOTA THANKED
THE WHITE BUFFALO CALF WOMAN
FOR THIS ABUNDANCE
○— BY CONTINUING ALONG —○
THE SACRED PATH
SHE HAD SHOWN THEM.

THE LEGEND OF
Popocatépetl
and the
Iztaccíhuatl

FROM THE NAHUA PEOPLE
OF MEXICO

The **Aztec Empire started** as three city-states in the Valley of Mexico: Tenochtitlan, Texcoco, and Tlacopan. The people were happy and prosperous. Their emperor, who ruled from the strongest city-state of Tenochtitlan, was a benevolent ruler beloved by all.

He and the empress had no children—although they had desired them for many years. This was the one sadness that hovered in the valley, for the people also wished for their emperor and empress to bear an heir for their great nation.

One day the empress came to the emperor with good news and a rounding belly: she was with child! The news spread throughout the valley, and joyful cries of "Congratulations!" popped like celebrations from one town to the next.

Several months later, the empress gave birth to a baby girl. She and the emperor named her Iztaccíhuatl—Izta, for short—and doted on her from the moment she was born. Izta grew up to be beautiful, both inside and out. Her face was flawless. Her hair flowed like ebony water-falls. And her smile

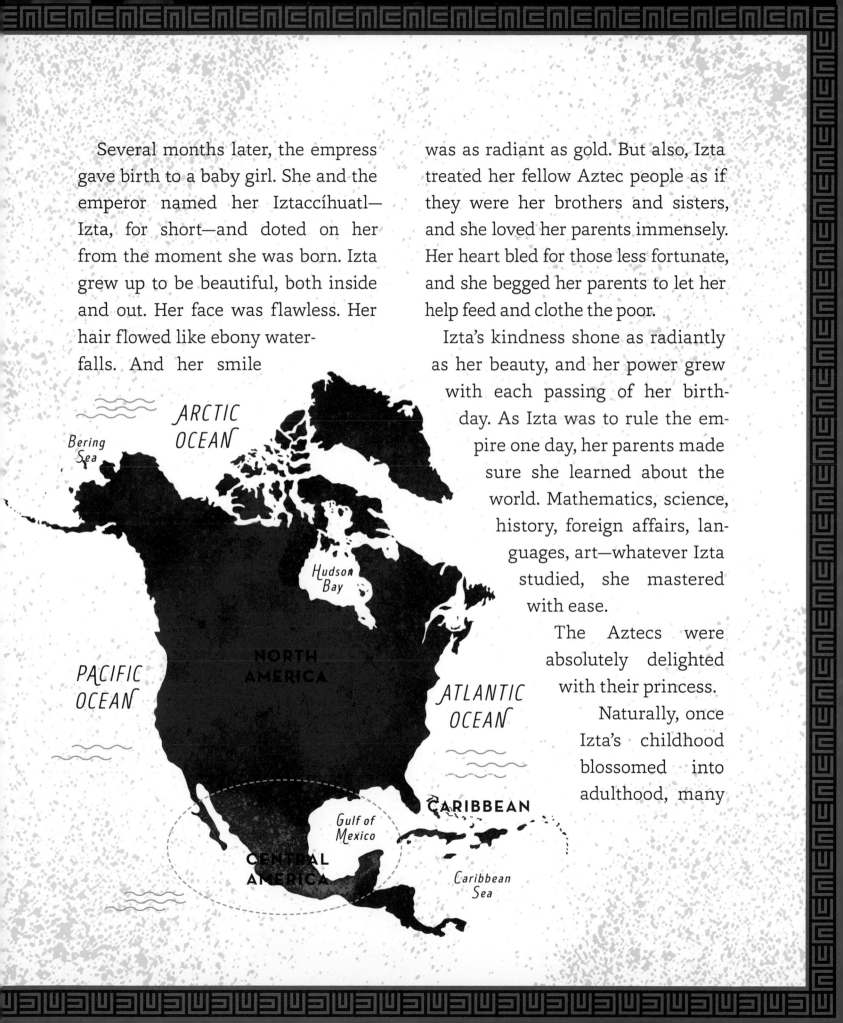

was as radiant as gold. But also, Izta treated her fellow Aztec people as if they were her brothers and sisters, and she loved her parents immensely. Her heart bled for those less fortunate, and she begged her parents to let her help feed and clothe the poor.

Izta's kindness shone as radiantly as her beauty, and her power grew with each passing of her birth-day. As Izta was to rule the em-pire one day, her parents made sure she learned about the world. Mathematics, science, history, foreign affairs, lan-guages, art—whatever Izta studied, she mastered with ease.

The Aztecs were absolutely delighted with their princess. Naturally, once Izta's childhood blossomed into adulthood, many men came knocking at the palace door to ask the emperor and empress for Izta's hand in marriage. But Izta had already fallen in love and told her parents who she wanted to marry. Her true love was Popocatépetl, a young Aztec warrior chief, the bravest and most handsome of them all. Izta was no fool—a princess was to have the best of everything, including a husband. The two had met and fallen madly in love. But while they spent many of their days together and dreamed about each other at night, war was brewing.

After many years of peace, in the neighboring city-state of Tlaxcala, an uprising was growing. The Tlaxcalan people had been angry with the emperor over the taxes he imposed on them, which grew costlier every year. They were tired of it and now refused to pay. There was even talk of their city-state splitting from the Aztec Empire, and the emperor wished to stop a rebellion before it began.

The emperor assembled his finest Tenochtitlan army to set out for battle. Popocatépetl—called Popoca—was the bravest of the chiefs as well as Izta's love. He was to lead the invasion.

"I know that you and my daughter wish to marry," the emperor said to Popoca. "If you are victorious in defeating our enemy, I will allow the marriage to happen. Bring me the head of the Tlaxcalan chief as proof of your victory, and we shall make it the centerpiece of your wedding feast!"

POPOCA WAS ENERGIZED
BY THE THOUGHT OF MARRYING HIS LOVE, IZTA.

He set out for Tlaxcala wishing to destroy his enemy and return home immediately. But plans do not always unfold the way we wish them to, and the war lasted many years. There were victories and losses. The whole time, Popoca kept Izta

in his heart and mind. The warrior missed his princess, and thought of her often.

During one especially fierce and bloody clash, it looked like Popoca was lost forever. A rival's sword went right through his thigh, and he fell to the ground in a heap. Popoca lay there for a very long time while his men pushed the enemy back. In the confusion of battle, a false message was too quickly sent back to the emperor, stating that Popoca had suffered a mortal wound in battle and had died. The message contained many details and was accompanied by a piece of Popoca's bloody armor, so the emperor had no reason to doubt it was true.

The emperor was crushed, and brought the news to the empress, not knowing how to tell their daughter.

"She will be devastated," said the empress. "I fear she may never recover from this news. But let me be the one to relay it. A mother has a special bond with her daughter."

So the empress went delicately to Izta and sat her in the most private room of the palace with a large picture window overlooking the rolling hills. She stroked her daughter's long, soft hair and spoke the words that Popoca, her love, had died in battle.

With this message, Izta opened her mouth to scream. But no scream made it out of her throat, and instead tears found their way. Izta's eyes overflowed as she doubled over in absolute pain, salt water running down her face. The tears flowed down her long, limp body and out the picture window, raining down on the empire.

Izta cried and cried and could not stop. No matter what her mother or father said to her, she kept on crying for her lost love. She could not eat. She could not sleep. Eventually, Izta died from sadness.

A CLOUD DARKENED THE WHOLE CITY-STATE OF TENOCHTITLAN,

whose citizens all mourned the loss of their fair princess and her love, Popoca.

The emperor and empress could

barely move themselves to lead the nation after their daughter's death. Cloaked in black, the two tried to comfort each other in their grief, but it was unmanageable. The only thing left to do was to give their beloved Izta an honorable burial worthy of their princess. All the efforts they would have put into planning her wedding, they now spent arranging her funeral.

It was the day the emperor and empress were prepared to bury their daughter. All the subjects of Tenochtitlan lined up behind their great leaders to follow the funeral procession of fair Izta, which was to stretch from the palace to the royal burial grounds in the hills. The long road out of the capital was lined with flower petals, and each citizen had placed a candle in their front window to pay their respects to the princess.

As the funeral procession began its slow march, they were met with a raucous, victorious group riding in from the opposite direction. It was Popoca, returning with his warriors, the rival chief's head in his satchel.

They had won the war! Popoca could not wait to tell the emperor and his beloved Izta. He had been dreaming of this day for many years.

What luck! Popoca saw the emperor and empress approaching him along the road. As he rode nearer, however, he saw their tear-streaked faces and their shrouds of black. Even nearer, Popoca saw shocked faces, stark white from their blood having drained from heads to toes.

"My emperor! My empress! We have won the war against the Tlaxcalan people. We have finally crushed their rebellion. They are and will forever be yours!" Popoca's noble leaders only stared at him with mouths agape.

"Where is my love, Izta? Where is my betrothed?" Popoca exulted. But his face fell as soon as he realized his joy was not matched. He felt a terrible rumble throughout his body, just beneath the surface of his skin.

"Your love, Izta, is dead," said the empress, as she lay a gentle hand on his armor. "We thought you were, too." And she told him, right there, of the eternal sadness that had befallen Izta when she thought Popoca was killed in battle. Popoca turned to look and saw the limp body of his beautiful princess, laid upon a platform covered in flower petals and vines.

In his grief, Popoca ran to her and kissed her face. It was just as soft and lovely as he remembered it. He steeled himself against the red-hot grief and rage now winding its way deep into his core. He wanted to enjoy his last few moments with Izta, so he instead focused on his love for her.

Popoca lifted her delicate body and carried her the rest of the way up into the hills, his warriors following along to support their chief. When the troupe arrived at the rolling green hills of the royal burial grounds, Popoca asked his men to build a funeral slab for her body.

"Make it smooth and sturdy, and collect some flowers as beautiful as she is," he instructed. When the funeral table was ready, Popoca lay Izta on top of it and scattered multicolored flowers over her body and face.

Then he ordered his men to leave him there, and they did as they were

told. Popoca had decided he would not leave Izta's side for the rest of his life. He lit his torch, for the sun was now setting on the dreadful day he had discovered his love was dead. Kneeling down to watch over Izta, Popoca died of sadness as well.

The Aztec gods were touched by the immense love between Popocatépetl and Iztaccíhuatl—they had seen nothing like it before. So they turned the bodies of Izta and Popoca into two great volcanoes, side by side, both of which can be seen today on the fringes of Mexico City.

The name *Popocatépetl* in Náhuatl means smoking mountain; true to its name, this volcano still smokes and rumbles occasionally.

WHEN POPOCATÉPETL BECOMES ACTIVE, THE LOCALS SAY IT IS POPOCA PROVING THAT HIS PASSION FOR IZTA STILL LIVES ON.

The Hero Twins Visit the Underworld

FROM THE MAYAN PEOPLE
OF MESOAMERICA

Long ago in the Mayan Empire, there were twins, Xbalanque and Hunahpu, who were very good at playing racquetball. It was part of their legacy, as their father and uncle had been expert ball players before them. The twins hit with precision. They dodged with lightning speed. They volleyed the rubber ball between them, laughing and shrieking in the garden of their grandmother's home. There, they lived carefree days and made a lot of noise. The boys' grandmother loved them and took care of them, despite all the commotion their ball games caused.

But they were not loved by all.

Like their father and uncle, the twins were so good and so noisy when playing ball that they greatly disturbed the Death Lords of Xibalbá. Xibalbá was another name for the underworld, where rivers flowed with blood and cavern walls bubbled with pus.

The Death Lords enjoyed nothing

more than breathing death into vibrant souls, especially when those souls were noisy and bothersome. So they summoned Xbalanque and Hunahpu to Xibalbá to come and play in their court.

The macabre invitation to the underworld landed at the twins' home. To their grandmother,

it was all too familiar. She had lost her own beloved twin sons, Xbalanque and Hunahpu's father and uncle, to Xibalbá when they were invited to play ball. History has a way of repeating itself, and naturally she did not want Xbalanque and Hunahpu to go. But she knew she could not keep them from accepting the invitation from the Death Lords of Xibalbá. It was mandatory, and so Xbalanque and Hunahpu prepared for their journey.

Their grandmother pulled the twins aside before they left home. "If you are to travel to Xibalbá," she instructed, "you must be aware of the many challenges that the Death Lords will throw your way. . . ." And she told the boys all she knew. The twins headed off for Xibalbá, carrying their rubber ball and their rackets with them.

THEIR FIRST TEST met them at the gates of Xibalbá: Which of the Death Lords were real, which were mannequins? Thanks to a helpful mosquito, the twins soared through this one. The mosquito stung each Death Lord and made some of them jump while others stood stone-still. Xbalanque and Hunahpu easily picked out the fakes.

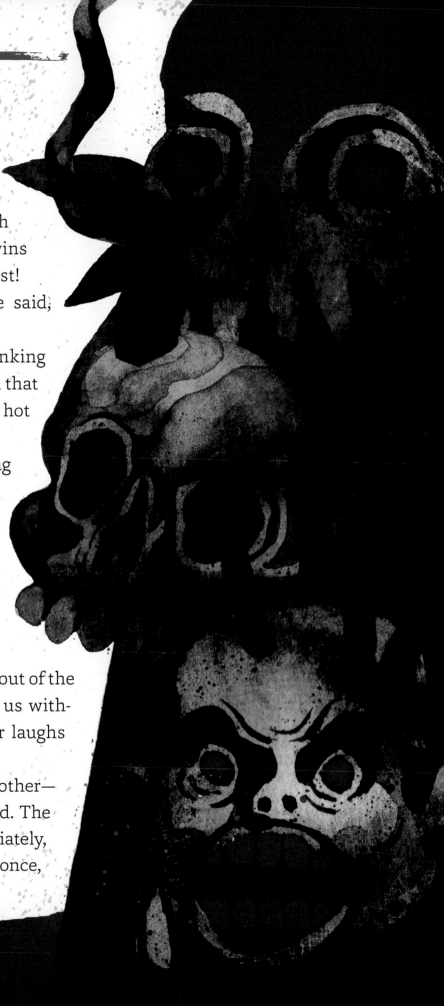

Impressed, the Death Lords welcomed Xbalanque and Hunahpu inside. Next, one of the Death Lords motioned for the boys to sit on a bench and rest after their long journey. The twins glanced at each other. It was another test!

"No, thank you, Lords," Xbalanque said, avoiding the seat.

"We will stand," added Hunahpu, winking at his brother. For the twins recognized that it was not a bench, but a flat and very hot cooking stone.

Now, the twins' cleverness was making the Death Lords angry. And you do not want to make a Death Lord angry!

"Into the Dark House you go!" the Death Lords shouted. And they kicked the boys into a maze-like house with no windows, black as midnight inside, and threw them a lit torch. "If you manage to find your way out of the house, this torch must be returned to us without a single inch burned down." Their laughs echoed throughout the underworld.

Xbalanque and Hunahpu had each other—and a plan—and so they were not afraid. The twins extinguished the torch immediately, so it would not burn any further. At once,

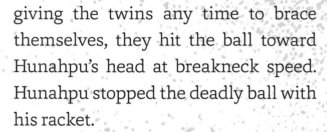

hundreds of fireflies flew from their pockets and landed where the flame once was, to light the boys' way to safety. When they emerged from the Dark House with the torch unburnt and intact, the Death Lords were furious.

The Xibalbáns then forced the boys through many different tests: a night in the Razor House, a night in the Ice House, a night in the Jaguar House, and then a night in the Fire House. Each test was more lethal than the last. Yet night after night, the boys came out victorious.

NOW IT WAS TIME FOR THEIR FINAL TEST:
THE BALL GAME!

The Death Lords' ball, which boasted a saw-like blade, sat in the middle of the court. Without

giving the twins any time to brace themselves, they hit the ball toward Hunahpu's head at breakneck speed. Hunahpu stopped the deadly ball with his racket.

"What is this?!" he cried out with foolish courage. "Your ball almost sliced my head off! We will only play a game that is fair and square . . . and with our ball."

"Fine, you can use your own ball," the Death Lords agreed. And so the twins played a long game against the Death Lords of Xibalbá. It was unlike any other they had played. The game skirted the boundary of fun and fear as the twins battled between life and death.

But sure enough, the twins—who truly were the best at playing ball—defeated the Death Lords in the game. Xbalanque and Hunahpu hugged, then grabbed each other's hands and ran far away from Xibalbá. In the distance, they heard the screeches of the Death Lord mob.

"Nobody beats Death and gets away with it!" they screamed. Heads aflame, they continued plotting the end of the twins.

Xbalanque and Hunahpu rejoiced, safe and sound at home with their grandmother—who was relieved her boys had returned. They became known throughout the land as the Hero Twins.

But they were not safe and sound for long. When the twins soon received another invitation to Xibalbá, they knew they'd continue to be summoned to meet the Death Lords until they died. No one, not even boys as clever and cunning as the twins, could cheat Death forever. So they made up their minds.

Once again, the twins journeyed to the underworld and met the Death Lords at the gates. They were not reluctant to enter, despite the gruesome smiles of the Xibalbáns beckoning them to their deaths. The twins found themselves in the middle of a circle of ghoulish figures all closing in on them.

"Welcome, welcome!" the Lords greeted them, inching nearer. "We challenge you to a new game, one you've never seen before. We think you clever boys will like this one the best! Come with us."

The Death Lords led them to an open pit. It was a ring of large stones with a high stack of branches and twigs in the middle. One of the Lords kindled the wood with his eyes, and the whole stack went up in a burst of flames. They licked the sky, reaching higher than the Death Lords, who were already much taller than the boys.

"We bet you cannot jump over our fire four times," they challenged Xbalanque and Hunahpu. The twins would not be fooled, and instead of attempting the trick, they jumped right into the flames and were consumed.

The Death Lords clapped and laughed around the fire. This sudden turn of events delighted them more than ever. They had fooled the boys and had finally succeeded in killing them. The Death Lords had earned their revenge for the embarrassing defeat on the ball court.

"Now, what to do with their ashes?"

they asked each other, drunk with power and giddy with death.

"Let's just toss them into the river," one shouted.

The Death Lords ceased the flames, collected the boys' ashes into a small can, and dumped it into the river without a care in the underworld. Then they walked away, thinking they'd never see the twins again.

What the Lords of Xibalbá did not realize, however, was that by throwing the ashes of Xbalanque and Hunahpu into the river, the boys were able to come back to life. First, the twins' ashes gathered into the form of two catfish. Eventually they turned back into themselves, the Hero Twins.

Even though Xbalanque and Hunahpu were themselves on the inside, they looked different on the outside. Now, they looked like travel-weary old men, wearing wrinkled faces and frayed rags. But despite their appearance, they were energetic and engaging—and fashioned themselves into street performers who put on outstanding shows.

They would burn items, like trees and houses, and then bring them back to their original states. They would turn themselves inside out, then back to normal. One twin would even destroy the other in front of a whole audience; then the dead one would jump back to life. The crowds were astounded.

Word of their act reached the Death Lords of Xibalbá, who immediately beckoned them to perform a special show. They did not know the performers were actually the twins, back from the dead.

"We have heard great things about you both," they said. "Pull out all the stops for us!"

First, the twins sacrificed a chicken and brought it back to life. The Xibalbáns clapped politely.

Next, they sacrificed a human and brought him back to life. The Xibalbáns were more interested now, leaning forward in their seats to see the show better.

"Do each other now!" the Death Lords shouted. So Xbalanque chopped up Hunahpu into small pieces until his twin was scattered all over the floor. Then Xbalanque called for Hunahpu to get up and dance. The pieces of Hunahpu gathered together in a mound, arranging themselves just so until the twin was upright and alive again. At Xbalanque's instruction, Hunahpu did a jaunty dance.

The Death Lords of Xibalbá could barely contain themselves. They burst into laughter and applause, and leaped from their seats shouting, "Do us now! Do us!"

Xbalanque and Hunahpu glanced at each other for a second, not long enough for the Death Lords to see. This is what they had returned for.

The two most powerful Death Lords now stood on stage between the performing twins, who brandished axes with honed blades that glinted in the firelight of Xibalbá. And in one clean swoop, the twins cut off the Death Lords' heads. The heads dropped to the ground with a thud and rolled to the feet of the audience of Death Lords. The twins did not move to bring the Lords back to life.

The performers took a slow bow and turned once in a full clockwise spin. When they met the eyes of the dead-silent crowd of Lords, they revealed their true faces: those of the young Xbalanque and Hunahpu.

"Remember who killed your two greatest Lords and defeated Xibalbá, once and for all," they shouted. "It was us, Xbalanque and Hunahpu, the Hero Twins!"

WITH THE DEATH LORDS FINALLY VANQUISHED AND THEIR QUEST COMPLETE, XBALANQUE AND HUNAHPU SOARED INTO THE SKY TO BECOME THE SUN AND MOON.

The Mapinguary

FROM BRAZILIAN MYTHOLOGY

The Amazon rainforest spans almost the entirety of Brazil, an enormous country. As the world's largest tropical rainforest, it contains more animals, insects, and plants than can even be counted. With dense trees tall enough that you cannot see their crowns, a canopy so thick that sunlight cannot penetrate, poison frogs, spiders as large as melons, prowling jaguars, and a million other creeping creatures, this wild and untamed landscape was home to Inocêncio, the best hunter and guide in all of Brazil. Many wealthy men from all over the Americas hired him to lead their expeditions around the Amazon's Urubu River. They didn't trust anyone else—only Inocêncio, since he was the smartest, the strongest, and the bravest hunter around. His crew of men would follow him into the darkest, most dangerous places.

But there was one thing—and one thing only—that made Inocêncio's body tingle with fear: **A BEAST CALLED THE MAPINGUARY.** Was the creature real? Was it a myth? Living in the rainforest, Inocêncio had heard many cautionary tales of strange beasts, both mythical and true. But gory narratives of the mapinguary

had haunted him as a little boy and still held fast to his most frightful fantasies. Even now, he shouted out in his sleep and awoke sweating from nightmares of the foul beast. One could say Inocêncio was obsessed.

Several trustworthy people had told him graphic, vivid accounts of the monster and the bloody carnage it reaped in the dead of night. The mapinguary was said to look like a giant sloth, but terrible and rabid. It walked on all fours, but when it encountered a man, it reared up on its

hind legs and became seven feet tall. Slow as molasses but also smart and ferocious, it could trick a man into dropping his weapons and freezing in place, turning even the greatest warrior into lowly prey.

Every account of the mapinguary described its features in the same way: **ONE LARGE, GLASSY EYE** that it used to stun its victims; **LONG, POINTED CLAWS** like giant machetes; **BLOOD-RED FUR** with a thick, scaly layer of bulletproof skin underneath; **AND TWO TERRIBLE MOUTHS**—one on its face and the other on its belly. That scared Inocêncio most—two mouths meant two chances to be devoured by the foul beast.

The mapinguary only ventured out at midnight. Sometimes it screamed in order to confuse its victims. But it could also remain silent as it slowly stalked the forest. However, it could not hide its stench, which had been known to make strong men weak and cloud their sane minds. The beast

was said to smell like decay and death, the mixed scent of rotten flesh, vomit, and excrement rising from its every pore.

No matter how hard Inocêncio tried to put on a brave face, there was little he could do to hide his fear of this terrifying figure.

Which is why his knees now shook uncontrollably, and cold sweat prickled his skin with goose bumps. It was darkest midnight and Inocêncio was somehow alone. That never happened—he was always with his crew. His men gravitated toward him, looking to him for instructions and security. Now, he was the person who needed help. Thankfully, his torch still glowed. But it was beginning to flicker.

Earlier that day, his group had spotted something rare and unsettling: four large and putrid-smelling footprints. Inocêncio had a nagging feeling that he knew exactly what had left

those giant tracks . . . and he was terrified.

Like a fool, he had trekked out at twilight to see those tracks again, telling his crew he'd be right back. But it had quickly grown dark, and suddenly Inocêncio was lost and in deep trouble.

Inocêncio kept his eyes and ears wide open and held his breath, trying to figure out what to do next. His torch threw spooky shadows on the trees. A tingle went up his spine, and he stilled himself.

Then he saw them: the same ghastly footprints from earlier in the day, but now there were more of them! Inocêncio gasped. When he kneeled down to get a closer look, the stench of death and decay tossed him backward. Inocêncio rubbed his nose, trying to rid it of what he knew he had smelled before . . . but only in his nightmares. That's when his fears were confirmed: these were the tracks of the mapinguary!

Inocêncio suddenly felt ill and dizzy. He placed his hand on his hunting rifle, although it was almost impossible to kill the mapinguary. His heart drummed like madness in his chest and his eyes began to twitch. Inocêncio tried to compose himself so he could escape, but then—

Bloodcurdling screams shook the forest! Inocêncio jumped three feet into the air and fell with a thud. The dreadful screams were constant, and closing in. Now the noise was all around him, full of deep, guttural grunts and repulsive slobbering.

Inocêncio shone his torch all around and tried running in every direction, but he could not find his escape. His scrambled mind and confused legs drove him right into the stomach of the mapinguary, where he came face-to-mouth with the beast!

"Ahhhhhh!" Inocêncio bounced off the hairy torso and dropped his torch, which was smothered, plunging both man and beast into total darkness. He scurried up the nearest tree as fast and as high as he could.

Inocêncio had narrowly escaped being devoured by the mapinguary.

But he was now stuck in the tree as the mapinguary bellowed and gurgled and screamed below him. The beast slashed and crashed around, scrabbling for Inocêncio, who clung with white knuckles to the tree's bark. Sweat streamed off his body, making the mapinguary even more ferocious. The mapinguary's screech became even wilder as it became angrier.

In the darkness, Inocêncio could hardly see a thing, but he felt his own fear rise with the screams and grunts coming from the mapinguary's two mouths. And—that smell! It was enough to make Inocêncio want to cut off his own nose. His tree began to quake as the smell got closer, closer, and closer . . . until Inocêncio felt hot, thick breath on his ankles. The mapinguary was climbing his tree! The hunter was now the hunted.

Inocêncio swung himself up to a higher branch. Several knife-like claws grazed his legs, so he reached for his rifle and fired several shots at the mapinguary. The beast's bloodcurdling scream echoed through the trees, and Inocêncio had to cover his ears. Suddenly, there was a thud and an eerie *scrape scrape scrape* across the jungle floor as the mapinguary seemed to slink away.

COULD IT BE TRUE?

Had Inocêncio wounded the beast? He had no more strength left to even ponder it. Inocêncio's eyes rolled back in his head, and he passed out.

The lingering smell of rotting flesh roused Inocêncio from a darkness blacker than black. This time he woke from his nightmare still clinging to the tree branch he had scrambled to the night before.

Inocêncio rubbed his aching neck. The beast was no longer beneath him. He was still shivering, and the pit of his stomach felt rotten. But he was alive. And he had seen the mapinguary!

"Inocêncio!" He heard a voice call in the distance. It was his crew!

Inocêncio called back and jumped down from the tree, landing in a giant muddy footprint, which splashed up as he landed. Immediately Inocêncio smelled the sour odor of the mapinguary over his whole body. He tried to wipe his hands, but there was blood everywhere. Inocêncio panicked again until he realized he was fine. The muddy footprint was filled with blood. Mapinguary blood. His whole body was covered in it. Inocêncio must have struck the beast with his bullets after all!

BUT IT HAD GOTTEN AWAY...

His men shouted his name again and ran to his side, holding their noses in disgust and fear. Inocêncio didn't even know where to begin to tell them what had happened, what he'd seen, and what he'd endured

He immediately declared their expedition over and led his men back home, quicker than he had ever trekked in his whole life.

FOR WHILE INOCÊNCIO HAD IMPOSSIBLY SURVIVED THE MAPINGUARY THIS TIME,

HE KNEW THE BEAST

STILL STALKED THE JUNGLE . . .

El Alicanto

The legend of el Alicanto is well known in Chilean culture, but one boy named Martín learned of this mythical bird the hard way. One morning, Martín woke up to the sound of trumpets blaring and crowds cheering in the near distance. It was still early, but the warm sunshine was reaching in through his small bedside window to pry open his eyes. His parents had already gone out, and the whole day stretched before him. Today was the start of Las Fiestas!

Pulling on his most colorful festival wear—a yellow T-shirt and shorts, as bright as flames and as flashy as gold—Martín hopped around his bedroom to the sound of the parade making its way down the main boulevard. He practiced some dance moves, too. One sock, two socks, *slide*. One shoe, both shoes, *slide*. There! Almost ready to go meet Joaquin and Max, who were probably already there with their older brothers and sisters, whooping it up with their faces painted and noisemakers in their hands.

One quick stop first: Mamà and Papà's top drawer, where Martín knew they stashed some money for emergencies. And this was an emergency, for sure. Martín needed enough coins to buy ice cream later in the day, and a new kite for the competition. He would be sure to pay them back afterward.

Martín looked all around him—

Caribbean Sea

NORTHERN SOUTH AMERICA

PACIFIC OCEAN

SOUTHERN SOUTH AMERICA

ATLANTIC OCEAN

even though he knew he was alone in the house—quietly opened the drawer, and rummaged through the socks until he found it: a sack of coins, golden and silvery and waiting to be dropped into the boy's pocket.

"Stop right there, mijo!" a stern voice exclaimed. Martín nearly jumped out of his dancing shoes! His short black hair stood on end for a second and he turned around slowly, knowing full well who the voice belonged to.

"Abuela . . . ," Martín addressed his grandmother. "I didn't realize anyone was here."

"Good thing I was here," she scolded, pointing her finger like something out of a Western film where Martín was the culprit and Abu was the sheriff who had caught him. "Put down that sack of coins that is not yours." Martín did as he was told, apologized, and began to back out the door.

"Not so fast, Martín," Abuela called. "Come here. Sit down with me."

"But, Abu! Joaquin and Max are—"

"I don't care where those silly boys are. You're with me now, and here you'll stay. I have a little story to tell you . . ." She raised her eyebrows and patted the seat next to her. Martín dragged his feet over, sat himself down, and puffed out a long, forceful breath. He couldn't believe he was missing all the fun.

"Don't pull that face on me either. El Alicanto wouldn't tolerate you as much as I am right now . . ."

Okay, here goes Abuela with another story, thought Martín, trying not to roll his eyes in front of her. *Hopefully this will be a quick one . . .*

"I must have told you about el Alicanto before, sí?" When Martín shook his head, she continued. "Ah, it is the symbol of good fortune for anyone who sees it—the young and old, the rich and poor, the honest and . . . greedy. Those who see it may come upon great wealth, but only if their intentions and hearts are pure.

"El Alicanto is a giant gilded bird with wings that span the length of a whole house. It's said that the bird's enormous wings are striped with silver, and its large curved beak and strong claws are fashioned out of gold.

Its head and

neck are shaped like a swan's: very fine and delicate. The bird's eyes give off quick flashes of light, like glinting jewels. And its tail makes sparks as it flies through the air.

"YOU'VE NEVER SEEN A CREATURE OF SUCH STUNNING BEAUTY!"

Martín shook his head, imagining this giant bird that could bring him wealth and happiness.

"El Alicanto lives in caves among the hills not too far from our desert town, where there are many deposits of precious metals like gold and silver. The bird lives nearby because it eats gold and silver to live. It hides most of the day, gobbling up riches. The color of its shine depends on whether the bird has eaten gold or silver—then it sparkles with the intensity of hundreds of golden bricks or silver necklaces. El Alicanto only ventures forth at night, and so it has no shadow or footprints to help people track it down. But when it glows gold or silver, a few lucky ones may see it.

"If the Alicanto has eaten a lot of precious metals, it will be slow and sluggish and must walk on land. But with an empty stomach—Dios mío!—it can fly faster than the wind."

"Whoa, that's pretty cool, Abu," said Martín, leaning forward now like a bird about to take off.

"Sí, it is, mijo. Very cool. El Alicanto can also hide easily to avoid being traced. If it senses that someone is following it—as many try to do, looking for riches—it can roll itself up in any small crack or crevice. Pretty sneaky, sí?"

"Yup. But has anyone actually seen el Alicanto?" Martín really wanted to know.

"Well, yes. But el Alicanto is the only one that decides who gets to see it. It's very protective of its food and will only share its gold and silver with those it deems worthy of it. So if you wanted to see el Alicanto—which I know you probably do—just wishing to see it or even pursuing it wouldn't help.

"And those who are after it must be careful! It has no tolerance for greedy people. So if it feels threatened in any way, its eyes will flash a brilliant light, blinding anyone who sees it. It has even been known to lead a greedy person off the edge of a cliff!"

Martín gasped and leaned backward in his chair so far that it almost tumbled over. Abuela shot out her hand to steady him. A cheer from the crowd outside tumbled into the house. Martín turned his head to the front door. He could just make out the sunlight glinting off the marching band instruments. The boy was itching to get outside, but the myth of el Alicanto still seemed unfinished.

"What else?" he said, and his abuela smiled. One of her gold teeth—his favorite one—flashed when she moved closer to him.

"Well, I'm sure you want to hear about the good stuff, sí?"

"Sí!"

"So if el Alicanto senses that a person has good intentions and a pure heart, it will actually lead them to gold and silver mines! It spits in the direction of where the precious metals are located: sputtering in gold if the deposit is gold, and in silver if the deposit is silver. Pretty clever, eh?

"So many people hope to see el Alicanto and benefit from its wealth. But only the ones truly deserving are fortunate enough to catch a glimpse. Even fewer follow it to riches.

"Do you see, Martín, why I scolded you for taking the money that wasn't yours?" Martín nodded slowly, his eyes dazzled by his grandmother's story. "Not only do greedy folks never get to see el Alicanto, but they may actually be harmed by it. Most importantly, those who are deserving will be led to good fortune, but you cannot be filled with a selfish spirit.

"And you are the most precious thing to me, querido. Truly. So please be a good boy—not just for me and el Alicanto, but also for your Mamà and Papà, who work so hard for this family. Keep your heart pure, like I know it already is."

Martín nodded again, even slower

this time, ashamed by his greed. He knew that if he had only asked nicely for some money the night before, his Mamà and Papà would probably have given it to him. Or he could have asked his friends to lend him some for the day.

Martín could not shake visions of giant flaming birds dancing in his head. They stomped and paraded in his mind. He swung his feet back and forth, back and forth to the beat of the big bass drums of the marching band.

"Looks like you've got dancing feet, mijo," Abuela said, flashing a gold tooth again. "Come, let us go to Las Fiestas together. Your Abu definitely knows how to dance!" She threw her arms up in the air, and Martín rolled his eyes—but also laughed.

"And you look like el Alicanto spit gold in your direction." She motioned to his flashy outfit. "Come, let's go get some ice cream. My treat."

Martín took Abu's hand once they got onto the jam-packed boulevard, both of them sweating among the crowd and shielding their eyes from the blinding sun.

"Abu, have you ever seen el Alicanto?" Martín asked.

"Yes, I have, mijo," she replied and winked, pulling her treasure in closer for a hug.

"SOMETIMES, EL ALICANTO'S REWARDS ARE EVEN GREATER THAN GOLD."

MYTHS OF ... THE ARCTIC

Tales from the Arctic span from its crackling, glowing skies to its dark and icy seas. They are full of mystery and traditions, woes . . . and powerful spirits who rule over all.

Sedna, the Mother of the Sea

FROM INUIT MYTHOLOGY

The Inuit say there is a woman who lives beneath the cold arctic waves. She is the mother of the sea, goddess of the underworld. She is the most important deity to the Inuit, as she rules over all sea creatures, which the Inuit depend upon for food and livelihood. She cannot abide hunters. She is angry and vengeful, but she can be appeased by shamans who swim to the seafloor to comb her silken hair. She must be pleased. She is Sedna.

As a child, Sedna grew up with a perpetual chill in her bones. She lived alone with her father, Anguta, in a dank igloo crusted with ice. It was cold where they lived, and they were very, very poor. But oh—Sedna was beautiful! Her face was strong, with two wide-set eyes that glittered like onyx, a bold nose set squarely between prominent cheekbones, and a mouth shaped like an elegant canoe. Her dark, silken hair flowed like it was constantly being stroked by the sea. Even wrapped in old, matted furs that kept her warm, she was radiant.

Anguta, on the other hand, had a face carved like a whittled piece of bark. His brow was gnarled and his nose, twisted. The spark in his eyes had dulled from too many years of frigid weather. What little hair he had left was as wispy and white as the arctic landscape. Sedna's father knew he wasn't getting any younger, and was anxious for his daughter to take a partner.

Many men came to propose to Sedna, but she was not interested. They were too ordinary for her, and she was looking for a life far improved from the bleak one she currently lived.

One day, a mysterious hunter suddenly appeared outside Sedna's family igloo. The man was dressed in fine furs, his neck dripping with charms

and souvenirs from his exploits, his eyes covered by tinted glasses made of an unknown tusk. The hunter appeared so exotic and otherworldly, he seemed to glide rather than walk. Sedna was enchanted, as the hunter took both her freezing hands in his.

"What is this fair beauty's name?" the hunter asked her with a voice like rushing sea winds. He rubbed her hands, and the friction between them instantly warmed her.

"My name is Sedna," she replied, gazing at his opaque eyes.

"Do me the honor of becoming my partner. I will make sure your life is luxurious for the rest of our days," he announced. "I will keep you warm and share with you all the meats from my hunting adventures. You will be comfortable and well-fed, I promise."

Sedna could not resist the hunter's proposal. The pair were a perfect match. Sedna agreed to marry him, and both she and her father were very pleased. The hunter carried her from her father's modest igloo into her new, promising life. As they left, Sedna's silken hair was whipped by the arctic wind, as if waving goodbye to Anguta and her old life.

Sedna and her new husband traveled long and far in order to return to the place where he lived. Enraptured with her new life, Sedna did not know exactly where the hunter was taking her. The whole journey became a thick fog in her mind.

When they arrived, Sedna was shocked to find the hunter had lied! There was no warm, lush life like he had promised. Instead the hunter stole her away into a crudely made—and freezing—shelter of moss and twigs. It was built into the side of a steep cliff on a barren island, which was completely deserted except for Sedna and the hunter. The wind whined above their heads and thrashed through the shelter as the violent sea waves crashed into the rocks below them. It smelled like rotting seaweed. Everything was gray and bleaker than where Sedna had come from, including the meager fish

the hunter tossed into Sedna's mouth, which was hanging open in shock.

"Where have you brought me? Who are you?" she cried and raged at her lying hunter-husband.

The man pulled off his tinted glasses, and Sedna gasped. His eyes were hideous and not human at all. Then the man removed his furs and Sedna screamed—he was not a man, but a terrible seabird! He was all claws and beak and forceful beating wings. The bird cackled in Sedna's face as she realized the full horror of the trick that he had played on her.

Sedna screamed again, then melted into sobs. The sound of her agony carried across the sea and to her father's ears.

"That is Sedna's cry!" Anguta said with alarm. He ran to his boat, barely leaving any time to pack a bag of provisions, and pushed off the icy shore in the direction of the cries. It took days for Anguta to arrive at the base of the rocky private island where Sedna and the seabird now lived.

"Father, I'm up here! Hurry!" Sedna

called down to Anguta when she saw him begin to scale the cliff to the nest where Sedna sat. Fortunately, they were able to escape because her seabird husband was out fishing. On the boat, rowing away from that dreadful island, Sedna told her father everything.

As Sedna finished recounting the shocking story to her father, a screech ripped through the air, loud enough to make their ears bleed. A blur of feathers and talons swooped by their heads and knocked them sideways. It was the seabird! He had spotted them rowing away, and nobody was going to steal his new wife and get away with it.

"Give me back my Sedna!" the seabird roared.

"No! My daughter will not be married to a liar and an ugly bird!" Anguta shouted back. Sedna began to shout obscenities at the bird, refusing to go back with him.

This twisted the seabird into a temper, and he flapped his wide wings so violently, it began to kick up the waves. The sky darkened, and the gust became a gale. Anguta's little boat started to toss and twist. The powerful bird had created a tempest out of his anger, and the sea whirled and swelled under his command.

"DO YOU DARE TO DEFY ME, OLD MAN?" THE SEABIRD SEETHED. "GIVE ME BACK MY WIFE OR I'LL KILL YOU!"

Anguta's blood pulsed loudly throughout his body, and he was sweating even in the freezing air. His boat rocked and began to split at the seams. The seabird raged on, stirring the storm into a tornado up above.

"I do not want to die," Anguta wailed as he panicked. "Here!" he shouted to the seabird as he threw Sedna out of his boat in desperation. It was a terrible impulse. But once he had done the deed, his blood turned cold and his mind turned mad.

Sedna's body stiffened as she tumbled overboard and plunged into the icy sea. Her shock was both a physical and mental anguish. At once she turned blue and bobbed between the waves, grasping for the side of her father's boat.

Anguta shouted at the wind and grasped his own neck as if he were choking. "I do not want to die, I do not want to die, I do not want to die…" he screamed over and over.

But the seabird would not stop. Sedna had managed to grip the canoe with long, frostbitten fingers.

"What are you doing on the side of my boat?" Anguta shouted to her. "And who are you, beast of the sea?" He looked at Sedna with crazed eyes. At once she knew he was no longer her father, but a madman. Before she

even had a moment to flinch, her father's knife came down quickly and cut off her fingers. Sedna slipped into the sea, her severed fingers dropping in after her.

The blood from her hands swirled in the violent water, morphing from red to black almost instantly. Sedna's blood grew thick and slick, and in its place, two seals bobbed their heads up on either side of hers. The seals then lowered back underwater and swam below.

The treacherous seabird quickened the deadly storm around them, and Anguta kept shouting into the void.

With hands stinging and heart aching from her father's blow, Sedna tried again to save herself from the incessant waves and the current trying to pull her under. She threw her bloody, dripping hands over the side of Anguta's boat once more and looked him straight in his maniacal, frightened face.

"Father, please help—" she began, but once again, Anguta gripped his knife and struck down, chopping off both her hands. Sedna slipped off the side of the canoe into the sea, each hand dropping with a splash. A gurgling cry came from beneath the water before she bobbed back up.

There was more blood coming from Sedna this time—also more pain and more distress. As the blood formed two giant pools on either side of her, Sedna felt delirious. Two enormous walruses emerged where the dark-red pools had been. The creatures then dove down to join the seals in the deep.

And, still, the deathly seabird hovered above, commanding the skies to destroy them both. From time to time, the bird would swoop down to try and grab his wife, but she was too slippery with water and blood.

Sedna was weak now, but still alive. She took one more chance and hurled her arms over the side of Anguta's canoe, latching on at the elbows. She pulled her body, shaking, out of the water for long enough to look Anguta in his blank eyes and whimper, "Father—"

But Anguta was quick, and wanted to be done with this. His arms moved swiftly, precise and efficient, for they were no longer his arms, but dastardly machines. Anguta stabbed his daughter in both wrists, opening her veins like he was breaking a dam. Sedna dropped down into the sea for the last time.

With her blood rushing out, Sedna stayed conscious for long enough to realize this was where she would meet her end. She clearly saw her father's face and the seabird's terrible eyes just before she dipped below the water's surface and everything blurred. As her body sank deeper and slipped into a gown of death, great whales emerged from the blood spilling from her arms.

Now the seabird was focused on his lost bride, dipping and shrieking at the surface of the sea, and Anguta was able to escape. The crazed man rushed away, kicking and thrashing through the water.

But Sedna had turned into a powerful sea goddess, having created some of the greatest and strongest creatures of the sea with her own living blood. She now reigned supreme on the ocean floor, with all the sea creatures obeying her every command. There she ruled over Adlivun, the Inuit underworld. And—by goddess!—was she seething with rage.

Sedna wanted revenge. Revenge against her father. Revenge against her false husband. And she would get it. The sea goddess conjured all the creatures that had sprouted from her body and blood.

"Fetch my wretched father and bring him to me," she said with a wry smile. "Take down that abominable seabird! I want them to pay." At once, every seal, walrus, and whale torpedoed toward the surface. The killer whale spotted the seabird perched on a rock and breached above the waves to grab his prey. He made sure to

eat the seabird in small bites, drawing out the death over many hours.

The rest of the sea creatures stormed Anguta's igloo, the power of the sea behind them. Waves swelled onto Anguta's land and thrashed against the old man's home. Before he could run away, seals restrained Anguta, dragged him out by his hands, and pulled him screaming into the sea. Walruses pushed him under and lugged him down to the underwater realm to meet his fate—face-to-face with his daughter.

"It's you! Daughter, please!" he begged. "I do not want to die, I do not want to die . . . !" he screamed over and over again, just as he had from his little boat. But this time only bubbles escaped his lips.

"MAKE NO MISTAKE: I AM NO LONGER YOUR DAUGHTER. I AM SEDNA, MOTHER OF THE SEA!"

Niekija
— and the —
Northern Lights

FROM SÁMI SHAMANISM

Imagine a sweeping, incandescent marvel of colorful lights in a dark night sky, swirls and flashes of green, pink, and violet that tumble like waterfalls of light from the heavens. These are the Northern Lights, or aurora borealis, a technicolor blanket between us on Earth and millions of stars.

In the snowy northern landscape live the Sámi, an ethnic minority and indigenous people whose territory spans Norway, Sweden, Finland, and Russia. The Sámi are well-acquainted with the harsh, frozen land and long winter nights—the perfect conditions for viewing the Northern Lights. The Sámi word for the Northern Lights is *guovssahasah*, meaning "morning and evening glow." It's only natural that this word does not distinguish between night and day, for it is a quarrel between Sun and Moon that explains its glowing presence . . .

Every day, the blazing Sun made his way across the sky in a golden chariot. He had many responsibilities: bringing life and sustenance to all who lived on Earth, making the plants grow, and shining down upon the Sámi people of the north so that they may be strong and prosperous. Sun had a son named Peivalke, who was broad, golden, and handsome, just like his father.

At twilight, Sun would finish his

ATLANTIC
OCEAN

Norwegian
Sea

NORTHERN
EUROPE

North
Sea

Celtic
Sea

EASTERN
EUROPE

WESTERN
EUROPE

SOUTH-
EASTERN
EUROPE

Black Sea

Mediterranean
Sea

Aegean Sea

daily arc by sinking below the horizon; at the same time, Moon would begin her ascent into the sky. The two would pass each other and nod. Then Sun would rest overnight to restore his powers for the next day.

That is when Moon would reign over the night with her silvery glow. She also had obligations to the Earth below her: making the ocean's tides rise and fall, illuminating the sky for nighttime travelers, and casting dreams into the minds of the Sámi people so that they may wake and chase those dreams. The Moon had a daughter named Niekija, who was graceful, radiant, and beautiful, just like her mother.

At dawn, it was Moon's time to rest, and she would bow out like a ballerina taking her final curtain call.

One afternoon as Sun was beginning his descent, Peivalke, his son, came to speak with him.

"Father, I am getting older and wish to marry. Who shall be my bride?" he asked.

"I will speak to the Moon this twilight. She has a beautiful daughter who would be the perfect bride for you, son." Peivalke agreed. The more Sun thought about this match, the more the idea made sense in his mind.

So as the celestial bodies made their exchange of day for night, Sun approached Moon.

"Moon, how is your beautiful daughter? From what I recall, she is as wondrous as you are," Sun said.

"Niekija is very well," Moon said, nodding with pride as she honed her glow for the night.

"My son, Peivalke, wishes to marry your fair daughter as soon as possible. What a perfect match this will be!" Sun said. But Moon's bright silver cast dimmed.

"No, no, no," the Moon shook. "She is only a child and is not yet ready for marriage. And anyway, your Peivalke is not worthy of my dear Niekija. He is brazen and fiery, and will surely scorch her if he gets too near. No, I will never allow it."

THE SUNSET PULSED WITH SHOCKS AND FLASHES OF LIGHT, AS SUN EXPLODED WITH RAGE.

······································

"How could you say this to me!? My son Peivalke is the worthiest in all the land! And Niekija will be his wife—I'll see to it myself!" Sun threatened as he blazed out of the sky.

Moon took Sun's threat seriously and wanted to protect her daughter, her most precious gift. That night as she hung in the sky, Moon sought out a place where Niekija would be safe from Sun and Peivalke. She spied a little green jewel of an island in the middle of the icy sea. It was wooded and secluded, with plenty of places to hide. And Moon could shine down on her every night and keep watch.

"That will be a safe place for my Niekija!" she thought, and sent her fair daughter there at once. Moon explained very little to her child except that she would cast a silver glow down on her every night, and that the girl was to find a place to hide from Sun during the day.

When Sun rose the next morning, he was still aflame with anger. The sea began to boil, the ice began to melt, and the air was sweltering. As Sun's chariot galloped its path through the sky, he looked for Niekija but could not find her anywhere.

But she was there, on that tiny island, hidden by dense forest. Niekija lived among the trees for several years, shielded from Sun's rage during the day, yet bathed in the glow of her mother's light at night. She even glimpsed the rare Northern Lights from time to time, that undulating and magical sight. Over time, and with Moon's nurturing gaze, Niekija grew into a dazzling young woman.

Sun did not let up in his quest for the young daughter of the Moon. In fact, his burning anger began to singe the tops of the trees on that little island where Niekija hid. The young woman knew the forest would no longer protect her from Sun. So she began to wander the island in search of a better place. And there it was: a rustic cabin on the shore. It was small and basic, but empty—the perfect place to hide away!

Niekija settled in and began to make the cabin a home. As the Moon's daughter, she possessed some of her mother's ethereal qualities. First, she drew the tide up and brought the sea inside so she could scrub the dirty floors and walls. Once that was done, she ebbed the tide and began to decorate the cabin, throwing moonbeams onto the ceiling until it glowed like an iridescent pearl. Then she cast images of her dreams onto the walls to keep her company. One wall boasted a picture of Niekija and her mother embracing, for she dreamed often of this reunion. Another wall depicted the glowing colors of the Northern Lights, which she considered more beautiful and mesmerizing than anything she had ever known before. Niekija also pinned up dreamscapes of herself in flight among the stars, bouncing along clouds, and racing with planets, asteroids, and other long-lost friends.

She finished as the afternoon settled into twilight, when she knew her mother would be rising. But instead of her mother's glow, Niekija saw something else shine through the small window of the little cabin: it was the Northern Lights! The lights grew closer and brighter, with colors more intense by the minute, until Niekija had to hide in a dark corner of the cabin.

Suddenly a giant warrior entered, his heavy footsteps pounding the nice, clean floors.

"What is this?" the man marveled. "My home is gleaming! And look at these pictures." The warrior gazed at Niekija's wondrous dreams on his walls.

"It's me . . ." the man said as he

examined the wall depicting the Northern Lights in all its glory. Niekija stepped out of hiding.

"Is that really you?" she whispered, and the man turned around. "Are you the Northern Lights?"

"Yes, my name is Nainas, and I am the Northern Lights," he said gently, already dazzled by her presence. "And are you the person who has made my small cabin into a warm home?"

"You are correct, I have done this. And I'm sorry—I didn't realize I had intruded upon your cabin. I am Niekija, daughter of the Moon," she replied, and told him the story of the Sun's rage and her exile to the tiny island where they now stood. "I have come here to hide, if you'll let me."

By the time Niekija had finished speaking, Nainas had fallen in love with her. In fact, he had fallen in love the moment he saw himself reflected in her dreamscape upon his wall. And Niekija already knew she loved Nainas the moment she had laid eyes upon him years ago, as the Northern Lights in the sky.

"Indeed, you may stay here forever. I will protect you, dear daughter of the Moon," Nainas replied. Niekija, so overwhelmed by the grace of this incandescent warrior, collapsed into his arms.

They embraced for a long time, as if they had known each other for years. Moon smiled down on the lovers, knowing in her heart that this was the right match for her daughter. When Nainas and Niekija finally pulled away and looked into each other's eyes, they knew they must always be together.

"Will you marry me, Niekija, daughter of the Moon?" he asked her, his voice crackling with electricity.

"Nainas, the Northern Lights, yes— I will marry you!" she replied, her silvery laughter illuminating the cabin's pearlescent ceiling. Mother Moon flickered her approval from the sky as the night quickly faded.

Nainas and Niekija's happiness shone in rays of light that emanated from every crack of that tiny cabin on the shore of the distant island.

Nainas began to burst with ripples of green, pink, and violet, and he could barely contain himself. He shone through the sky as the Northern Lights . . . alerting Sun to exactly where they were and what had happened.

"How dare you!" Sun boomed at Nainas, pinning him with a ray of light to the roof of his own cabin. Sun was scorching Nainas, and Niekija flew to her lover's side to stop it.

THIS WAS WHAT SUN WAS WAITING FOR!

He grabbed Niekija and cast Nainas into the heavens to glow for eternity, far away.

"Pievalke!" Sun shouted to his son. "Come, I have captured her for you!" Niekija writhed and screamed in Sun's grasp as he began to burn her skin.

When Pievalke arrived, Niekija shouted, "I will never marry you!" She faded into a silvery mist, evaporating in the presence of Sun and his son. Eventually Niekija slipped away to rejoin her mother, and now surrounds Moon with an otherworldly glow.

And so Niekija, daughter of the Moon, must watch from afar each night as her love, Nainas, glows as the Northern Lights.

NAINAS SHIFTS FROM GREEN TO PINK TO RED, UNDULATING WITH COLOR TO SIGNIFY HIS ENDLESS LOVE FOR NIEKIJA.

Special thanks to our international researchers, whose initial work
in gathering the stories became the basis for this book and enabled
the author to bring these myths and legends to life.

Many of these narratives were passed down in oral traditions, and have
multiple variations across different regions. In both the illustrations and the text,
the creators of this book have offered their own artistic interpretations
while making every effort to stay faithful to the heart of each story.

ACKNOWLEDGEMENTS
Publishing Director: Piers Pickard / Publisher: Hanna Otero
Editor: Rhoda Belleza / Art Director: Ryan Thomann
Designer: Marikka Tamura / Print Production: Lisa Ford
Author: Alli Brydon / Illustrator: Julia Iredale

Published in October 2019 by Lonely Planet Global Limited
CRN: 554153 / ISBN: 978-1-78868-308-1
www.lonelyplanet.com/kids
© Lonely Planet 2019
Illustrations © Julia Iredale 2019
4 6 8 10 9 7 5 3
Printed in Singapore

The artwork for this book was created with gouache, ink, and digital mediums.

STAY IN TOUCH - lonelyplanet.com/contact
IRELAND Digital Depot, Roe Lane (off Thomas St), Digital Hub, Dublin 8, D08 TCV4, Ireland

MIX
Paper from
responsible sources
FSC® C021741
www.fsc.org

Paper in this book is certified against the
Forest Stewardship Council™ standards.
FSC™ promotes environmentally responsible,
socially beneficial and economically viable
management of the world's forests.